KSSG–OKS

BAND II / VOLUME II
HAUS 10 / BUILDING 10

HERAUSGEGEBEN VON / EDITED BY
Marko Sauer und Christoph Wieser

MIT BEITRÄGEN VON / WITH
CONTRIBUTIONS BY
Georg Aerni, Florian Brunner, Urs Buschor,
Lorenzo De Chiffre, Clementine Hegner-van Rooden,
Fawad Kazi, James Licini, Marko Sauer,
Silvan Schneider, Christof Stäheli, Christoph Wieser

FAWAD KAZI II
KSSG–OKS
KANTONSSPITAL ST.GALLEN   OSTSCHWEIZER KINDERSPITAL

PARK BOOKS

INHALT		CONTENTS	

04 VORWORT
Marko Sauer, Christoph Wieser

06 EINE SUBTILE ROHFORM
Lorenzo De Chiffre

24 VOM MASTERPLAN ZUR MODULAREN NUTZUNG
Das Departement Bau und Raum KSSG im Interview
Urs Buschor, Marko Sauer, Silvan Schneider, Christof Stäheli

36 DER KONTEXT BESTIMMT DEN ENTWURF
Clementine Hegner-van Rooden

44 DAS ZEN DES STAHLS
Fawad Kazi, James Licini, Marko Sauer

52 DOKUMENTATION HAUS 10
Fawad Kazi

60 KSSG–OKS ECKDATEN
62 Biografien
64 Impressum, Dank

05 FOREWORD
Marko Sauer, Christoph Wieser

06 A SUBTLE RAW FORM
Lorenzo De Chiffre

24 FROM MASTER PLAN TO MODULAR USE
The Department of Building and Planning of KSSG in Interview
Urs Buschor, Marko Sauer, Silvan Schneider, Christof Stäheli

36 CONTEXT DETERMINES DESIGN
Clementine Hegner-van Rooden

44 THE ZEN OF STEEL
Fawad Kazi, James Licini, Marko Sauer

52 DOCUMENTATION BUILDING 10
Fawad Kazi

60 KSSG–OKS KEY DATA
62 Biographies
64 Imprint, Acknowledgments

VORWORT

Auf dem Areal des Kantonsspitals St.Gallen (KSSG) sind grosse Veränderungen im Gang: Über die nächsten sieben Jahre werden für das KSSG und das Ostschweizer Kinderspital (OKS) umfangreiche Erweiterungs- und Neubauten realisiert. Die Parkanlage mit Einzelbauten wird in einen zusammenhängenden Gebäudekomplex transformiert, der den städtebaulich wichtigen Grüngürtel entlang der Rorschacher Strasse unberührt lässt. Das in Etappen ausgeführte Bauwerk beinhaltet Erweiterungen für das KSSG und einen Neubau für das OKS, das als eigenständiges, aber räumlich und betrieblich optimal eingebundenes Spital funktionieren wird.

Der zweite Band der fünfteiligen Buchreihe KSSG–OKS ist dem Haus 10 gewidmet. Dieses Gebäude liegt ganz im Norden der Spitalanlage und beherbergt die Klinik für Psychosomatik, die Endokrinologie/Diabetologie, die Ernährungsberatung sowie die Ambulatorien Nephrologie/Hämodialyse und Onkologie/Hämatologie. Ein ausgeprägter Höhenversatz und die Lindenstrasse trennen es vom restlichen Areal, mittels einer zweigeschossigen Passerelle schliesst es dennoch an das Wegenetz und die Versorgungskanäle des Spitals an.

Die Belegung mit Kliniken, Ambulatorien und Grossraumbüros ermöglichte es dem Planerteam, seine konzeptionellen Annahmen zu schärfen, bevor mit den Häusern 07A und 07B sowie dem OKS die grossen Neubauten realisiert werden. Im Fokus standen dabei die Anwendung eines einheitlichen Konstruktionsrasters für unterschiedlich grosse Behandlungs- und Untersuchungszimmer sowie Labore und Administration. Hinzu kam der Umgang mit einer sich rasant verändernden Gebäudetechnik und den Anforderungen der Medizin, die ebenfalls einem steten Wandel unterworfen sind. Diese Aspekte konnten die Betreiber des Kantonsspitals für ihre weitere Planung überprüfen und verifizieren.

Bezüglich Ausdruck und Atmosphäre erlaubte das Projekt dem Architekten Fawad Kazi einige Freiheiten: Da das Haus 10 ein wenig abseits des Areals steht, konnte er im Ausdruck des Gebäudes einen spezifischen Ansatz verfolgen. Während die Neubauten auf dem Hauptareal in einem sichtbaren Kunststein ausgeführt werden sollen, zeigt Haus 10 eine Verkleidung aus eloxierten Aluminiumblechen. Und dank der riesigen Dieselmotoren der Netzersatzanlage im Erdgeschoss hat das Gebäude ein markantes Volumen erhalten: Die aus der Mantellinie tretenden Lüftungsschächte und der Schornstein auf der Westseite – beide unter demselben Kleid aus Aluminium mit dem restlichen Haus vereint – verleihen dem Gebäude eine unverwechselbare Silhouette.

Marko Sauer und Christoph Wieser

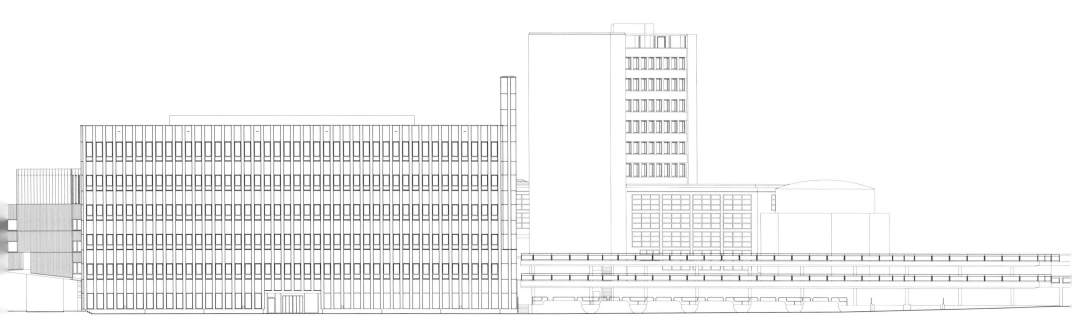

FOREWORD

Major changes are taking place on the grounds of the Cantonal Hospital St.Gallen (KSSG): extensive expansions and new structures will be created for the KSSG and the Children's Hospital of Eastern Switzerland (OKS) over the next seven years. The park, with its individual buildings, will be transformed into a coherent complex without affecting the green belt along Rorschacher Strasse, which is a crucial urban planning element. The overall structure, being built in stages, includes expansions for the KSSG and a new building for the OKS. The new building will function independently but will be optimally integrated within the hospital grounds and operations.

The second volume of the five-part book series KSSG–OKS is dedicated to Building 10. This building is located in the far northern area of the hospital complex and houses the clinics for psychosomatics, endocrinology/diabetology, nutrition counseling, and also the outpatient clinics for nephrology/hemodialysis and oncology/hematology. While a pronounced jump in height and Lindenstrasse separate it from the rest of the grounds, a two-story aerial walkway connects it with the hospital's network of routes and supply ducts.

The configuration of clinics, outpatient clinics, and open-plan offices allowed the planning team to refine its conceptual assumptions prior to realization of the major new structures, Buildings 07A and 07B as well as the OKS. For this, the focus was on implementation of a uniform construction grid for differently sized treatment and examination rooms, as well as laboratories and administration. Added to this was dealing with a rapidly changing building technology and the demands of medicine, which are likewise subject to constant change. Those running the Cantonal Hospital were able to review and verify these aspects for their further planning.

The project allowed the architect Fawad Kazi several liberties in terms of expression and atmosphere: since Building 10 stands a bit apart from the grounds, he was able to pursue a specific approach for the building's expression. While the new building on the main grounds will be realized in visible cast stone, Building 10 reveals a cladding of anodized aluminum sheet. And the building has a striking volume thanks to the huge diesel motors of the emergency power system in the ground floor: the ventilation shafts that protrude from the surface line, and the chimney on the west side—both united with the rest of the building under the same dress of aluminum—lend the building a distinctive silhouette.

Marko Sauer and Christoph Wieser

Kantonsspital St.Gallen, nördliches Areal / Cantonal Hospital St.Gallen, northern grounds
1
Ansicht Nordwest 1:500 / Northwest view 1:500
2
Ansicht Nordost 1:500 / Northeast view 1:500

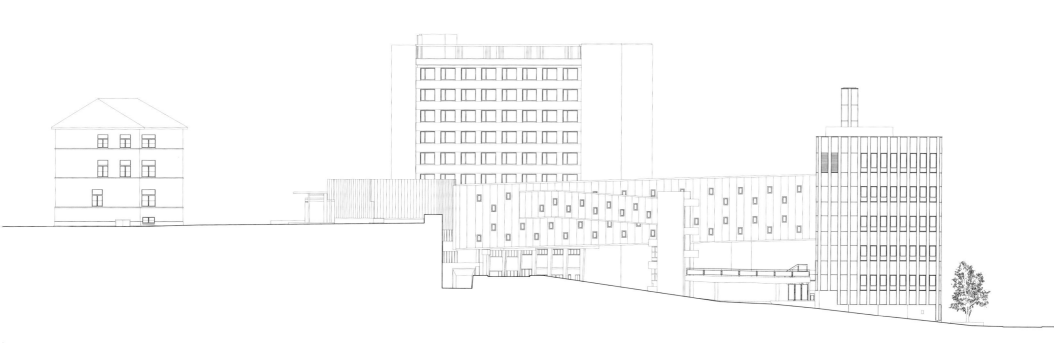

EINE SUBTILE ROHFORM
Lorenzo De Chiffre

A SUBTLE RAW FORM
Lorenzo De Chiffre

Kantonsspital St.Gallen, nördliches Areal /
Cantonal Hospital St.Gallen,
northern grounds
Foto / Photo: Florian Brunner

In den vergangenen zehn bis fünfzehn Jahren ist in St.Gallen eine beeindruckende Zahl an öffentlichen Neubauten entstanden. Etliche neue Verwaltungsbauten wie das Bundesverwaltungsgericht, das Verwaltungszentrum am Oberen Graben, die Erweiterung des kantonalen Hochbauamts sowie das Amt für Verbraucherschutz und Veterinärwesen verteilen sich über das Stadtgebiet. Auch mehrere Bildungsstätten, etwa das Bibliotheksgebäude der Kantonsschule am Burggraben, die Fachhochschule und die Primarschule St.Leonhard haben ebenfalls neue, architektonisch hochwertige Gebäude erhalten. Als Beobachtung am Rande ist auffallend, dass diese Bauten nicht nur das konstruktive, sondern auch das materialästhetische Repertoire des Betons auf unterschiedlichste Weise ausreizen. Die Stadt St.Gallen, einst bekannt für hochwertige Textilien, hat sich heute zu einem Betonzentrum entwickelt, wo sich in Gehdistanz ein Spektrum von raffiniertesten Betonanwendungen bewundern lässt.

Die sich im Bau befindliche Spitalerweiterung der Planergemeinschaft PG KSSG–OKS, unter Federführung des Architekten Fawad Kazi, wird sich als neuer Vertreter in diese eindrückliche Reihe von öffentlichen Bauprojekten einschreiben. Aber im Vergleich zu den oben erwähnten Bauten weisen die Erweiterung des Kantonsspitals St.Gallen und der Neubau des Ostschweizer Kinderspitals eine aussergewöhnliche Komplexität und Bauzeit auf, und sie sprengen den üblichen Massstab – ein Generationenprojekt.

EINE STADT IN DER STADT

Das Spital lässt sich mit einer Stadt in der Stadt vergleichen, die ständig erweitert und umgebaut wird. Übergeordnet gesehen ist es somit irreführend, von einem einzelnen Spitalerweiterungsprojekt zu reden. Viel eher handelt es sich um eine Vielzahl von unterschiedlich grossen, miteinander verbundenen Teilprojekten. Neben dem zentralen Erweiterungsprojekt sind in den letzten Jahren mehrere eigenständige Bauvorhaben am Kantonsspital St.Gallen umgesetzt worden, darunter der von Silvia und Reto Gmür konzipierte Neubau für Pathologie und Rechtsmedizin. Auch das sogenannte Haus 10, das im vorliegenden Band behandelt wird, zählt zu dieser Gruppe von Neu- und Umbauten. Gleichzeitig ist es auch der zweite Baustein in der Vorbereitung auf das Hauptprojekt und hat eine wichtige logistische Funktion für die Abwicklung des Grossprojekts. Zudem dient der vergleichsweise kleine Bau als Probelauf und Modell, in dem bauliche und organisatorische Abläufe für das zukünftige Hauptprojekt geprüft werden können.

Over the past ten to fifteen years, an impressive number of new public buildings have gone up in St.Gallen. Several new administrative buildings are scattered across the urban area, such as the Federal Administrative Court, the Oberer Graben Administrative Centre, the expansion of the Cantonal Building Department, as well as the Office for Consumer Protection and Veterinary Affairs. Several educational facilities also have new buildings of the highest architectural quality, such as the school library of the Kantonsschule am Burggraben, the University of Applied Sciences, and the St.Leonhard Primary School. As a side remark, it is notable that these buildings make full use of not only the structural, but also the material-aesthetic repertoire of concrete in various ways. The city of St.Gallen, once known for high-quality textiles, has now evolved into a concrete center where a full spectrum of highly sophisticated concrete applications can be admired within walking distance.

The hospital expansion by the planning group PG KSSG–OKS, led by architect Fawad Kazi, which is currently under construction, will inscribe itself as a new representative within this impressive series of public building projects. However, compared with the previously mentioned buildings, the expansion of the Cantonal Hospital St.Gallen and the new building for the Children's Hospital of Eastern Switzerland display an extraordinary complexity and extended construction period, far beyond the usual scale—a project spanning generations.

A CITY IN THE CITY

The hospital can be likened to a city within a city, which is constantly being expanded and rebuilt. Viewed at a macro level, it is therefore misleading to speak of a single "hospital expansion project." Instead, at issue are a great number of interconnected partial projects of different sizes. In addition to the central expansion project, in past years several independent building projects have been realized at the Cantonal Hospital St.Gallen, including the new building for pathology and legal medicine designed by Silvia and Reto Gmür. The so-called Building 10, which is discussed in the present volume, is a part of this group of new buildings and conversions. At the same time, it is also the second building block in preparation for the main project and assumes a key logistical function in the handling of the large project. Additionally, the relatively small building serves as a trial run and model, in which constructional and organizational processes can be tested for the future main project.

Fawad Kazi, Kantonsspital St.Gallen, Pavillon, 2016–2017 / Fawad Kazi, Cantonal Hospital St.Gallen, pavilion, 2016–2017
Foto / Photo: Georg Aerni

In der Wettbewerbsphase waren zwei Provisorien in anderer Lage vorgesehen, die am Ende der Bauphase zurückgebaut worden wären. Erst im Laufe des Prozesses kam die Idee auf, ein einziges Rochadegebäude am nördlichen Rand des Spitalgeländes anzuordnen. Wohl wissend, dass solche Einrichtungen oftmals länger stehen bleiben als geplant, hat man im Sinne der Nachhaltigkeit entschieden, ein vollwertiges Gebäude zu errichten, das auch über die Bauphase hinweg Bestand hat. Und mit dem Ziel, die Zahl der Umzüge innerhalb des Spitals möglichst gering zu halten, hat auch das Haus 10 selbst einen Wandel durchgemacht: Statt Platz für Rochaden zu bieten, beherbergt es nun auf längere Zeit die Klinik für Psychosomatik, die Abteilungen für Endokrinologie, Diabetologie und Ernährungsberatung sowie die Ambulatorien für Nephrologie, Hämodialyse, Onkologie und Hämatologie.

PAVILLON

Der sogenannte Pavillon der Krankenhauskantine, der im ersten Band der Buchreihe ausführlich behandelt wurde, ist der eigentliche Auftakt des Grossprojekts. Hier, zwischen den beiden bestehenden Grossbauten (Haus 03 und 04), wurde der erste Teil des Generationenprojekts als kleines Passstück in die bestehende Spitalstruktur eingefügt.

Getragen von zwei pylonartigen Ortbetonstrukturen – eigentlich Rauchfänge für die im Untergeschoss verborgene neue Trafostation –, überspannt ein weiss gestrichener I-Trägerrost einen hellen, wintergartenähnlichen Raum. Trotz der bescheidenen Grösse sind hier mehrere Motive aus Fawad Kazis Architektursprache vorzufinden: eine tektonische Überformung der Verbindung zwischen tragenden und getragenen Bauteilen, wie etwa die würfelartigen Konsolen, die den Trägerrost stützen; ein unverhülltes Deckenbild, in dem haustechnische und konstruktive Systeme in ihrer Überlagerung ein abstraktes Webmuster bilden; die Verwendung von technischen Anlagen als gestaltgebendes Element. Dieser körperhafte Zugang zum konstruktiven Gestalten wird mittels Farbgebung zusätzlich betont. So ist alles, was die Erde berührt, in dunklen Farben gehalten, während alles, was von oben nach unten kommt, weiss gestrichen ist.

Betrachtet man den Pavillon als Destillat von Kazis persönlichem Architekturverständnis, könnte man an dieser Stelle auch seine Faszination für Orientteppiche und Pergamentlampen erwähnen. Diese traditionell-ornamentalen Artefakte, die man nicht spontan mit dem abstrakten Vokabular seiner Bauten in Verbindung setzen würde, verkörpern bei genauerer Betrachtung zentrale Semper'sche Themen, die für Kazis Werk wichtig sind. Gottfried

Foreseen in the competition phase were two provisional structures in a different location, which would have then been dismantled at the end of the building phase. The idea to place a single highly flexible building at the northern border of the hospital grounds first arose as the process unfolded. Knowing full well that such arrangements often remain longer than planned, and with an eye toward sustainability, a decision was made to erect a full-fledged building that would also remain standing beyond the building phase. And with the goal of keeping the number of moves within the hospital to a minimum, Building 10 has also gone through a transition: rather than providing a space for changing positions, it is now the long-term accommodation for the clinic for psychosomatic medicine, the departments for endocrinology, diabetology, and nutrition counseling, as well as the outpatient clinics for nephrology, hemodialysis, oncology, and hematology.

PAVILION

The pavilion that houses the hospital restaurant, which was discussed in detail in the first volume of the book series, actually sets the starting note for the larger project. This first part of the generational project was integrated like a small adaptor into the existing hospital structure between the two large buildings (Buildings 03 and 04).

Carried by two pylon-like in situ concrete structures—actually chimneys for the new transformer station concealed in the basement—a white-painted I-support grid straddles a bright, winter-garden-like space. Despite the modest size, several motifs from Fawad Kazi's architectural language are present: a tectonic transformation of the connection between load-bearing and supported building parts, such as the cube-like consoles, which carry the support grid; a bare ceiling in which the installation and construction systems overlap to form an abstract web pattern; and technical mechanisms used as design elements. This corporeal approach to structural design is additionally emphasized by the coloring. Everything that touches the earth is thus kept in dark colors, while everything that goes from top to bottom is painted white.

Viewing the pavilion as a concentrate of Kazi's personal approach to architecture, here we could also mention his fascination with oriental carpets and parchment lamps. Upon closer observation, these traditionally ornamental artifacts that would not spontaneously be associated with the abstract vocabulary of his buildings embody central themes of Gottfried Semper's

Kamelhautlampe, Pakistan, 1970er Jahre / Camel skin lamp, Pakistan, 1970s
Foto / Photo: Fawad Kazi

Semper beginnt bekanntlich sein wegweisendes Werk *Der Stil in den technischen und tektonischen Künsten oder praktische Ästhetik*[1], mit der Beziehung der textilen Kunst zur Baukunst. Einerseits werden hier Teppich bzw. Flechtwerk als raumbildende Elemente behandelt, andererseits werden die detaillierten Techniken des Webens, Knüpfens und Windens als Ursprung für tektonische Verbindungen genannt. Auch die Fassade als Kleid und das Prinzip des Stoffwechsels sind für die hier verfolgten Argumentationen zentrale Begriffe, die sich auf Semper zurückführen lassen. Ausserdem können die Pergamentlampen mit ihrer über ein Traggerüst gestülpten Kamelhaut in metaphorischem Sinn als Konzeptmodelle für Kazis Bauten gesehen werden. Wie im Folgenden dargestellt, sind diese von Semper beschriebenen Verknüpfungen mit der textilen Kunst auch im Haus 10 auffindbar.

PASSERELLE

Das Haus 10 steht am nördlichen Perimeter des Spitalgeländes – am weitesten vom Haupteingang entfernt und zwischen Service- und Infrastrukturbauten gelegen. Parallel zur Autobahn gerichtet, nimmt das Gebäude den mehrgeschossigen Niveausprung zwischen der Steinachstrasse und der höher gelegenen Lindenstrasse auf. Die Anbindung an die umliegenden Spitalbauten und das unterirdische Wegenetz erfolgt über eine Passerelle, eine 8 Meter hohe und 60 Meter lange, zweigeschossige Verbindungsbrücke, die im dritten und vierten Obergeschoss mittig von der südlichen Fassade aus an das Spitalgelände anschliesst.

Dieses zweigeschossige Bauwerk, das wie eine Nabelschnur das Rochadegebäude mit dem restlichen Spital verbindet, war aus technischer Sicht eine besondere Herausforderung. Eingekeilt zwischen zwei bestehenden Bauten auf der oberen Ebene teilt sich die Passerelle vom Areal aus gesehen nach etwa einem Drittel der Länge: Der Nebenzweig schliesst an eine bestehende Treppenanlage an, während der Hauptteil fortgeführt wird, um am Neubau anzudocken. Von aussen betrachtet unterstreichen die versetzten Fensteröffnungen die abstrakte Erscheinung des silbernen Brückenbaus. Im Inneren bilden die abwechselnd hoch und tief gesetzten Fenster eine kinematografische Folge von Ausblicken, die die Horizontlinie zu verwischen scheinen. Die raumhaltigen, schwarz lackierten Fachwerkträger sowie der rote Bodenbelag verstärken diese pulsierende Zick-Zack-Bewegung farblich. Im übertragenen Sinn lässt sich eine Verwandtschaft zwischen Passerelle und Restaurantpavillon – in Anlehnung an die obige Interpretation von der Pergamentlampe als Konzeptmodell – herleiten. In beiden Bauten werden die Stahlkonstruktionen ausnahmsweise

architecture that are key in Kazi's work. Gottfried Semper famously begins his pioneering work, *Style in the Technical and Tectonic Arts; Or, Practical Aesthetics*[1] with the relationship of the textile arts to architecture. On the one hand; carpets and wickerwork are treated as space-defining elements, on the other hand, the detailed techniques of weaving, tying knots, and coiling are cited as the origin of tectonic connections. The façade as dress and the principle of metabolism, which can be traced back to Semper, are also central concepts in the argumentation pursued here. Apart from that, the parchment lamps with their camel skin propped over a supporting structure can be seen in a metaphorical sense as conceptual models for Kazi's buildings. As will be presented in what follows, these links with textile art as described by Semper are also detectable in Building 10.

AERIAL WALKWAY

Building 10 is located on the northern perimeter of the hospital grounds—furthest from the main entrance and situated between the service and infrastructure buildings. Oriented parallel to the highway, the building absorbs the several-story jump between Steinachstrasse and the higher-situated Lindenstrasse. The connection to the surrounding hospital buildings and the underground network of routes occurs via an aerial walkway: an 8-meter-high and 60-meter-long, two-story connecting bridge, which connects to the hospital grounds from the center of the southern façade on the third and fourth floors.

This two-story structure, which like an umbilical cord connects the flexible-use building with the rest of the hospital, was a particular challenge from a technical standpoint. Wedged between two existing buildings, from a ground view the aerial walkway splits off on the upper level after roughly one-third of the length: an offshoot links up with an existing stairway, while the main section continues to then dock onto the new building. Viewed from outside, the offset window openings underscore the abstract look of the silver bridge structure. Inside, the alternating high- and low-set windows form a cinematographic succession of views, which seem to blur the line of the horizon. The black-painted spatial latticework truss and red floor intensify this pulsating zigzag movement through their coloring. In a figurative sense, a relationship can be deduced between the aerial walkway and restaurant pavilion—based on the above interpretation of the parchment lamps as conceptual model. In both buildings, the steel constructions are articulated as legible skeletons, as exceptions. In comparison with the larger buildings they seem

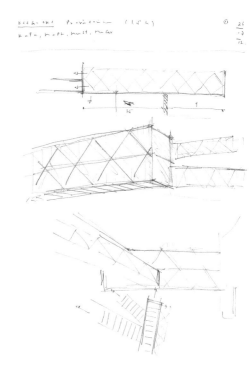

Fawad Kazi, Skizzenblatt A4, Bleistift, 26.07.2012 / Fawad Kazi, A4 sketch, pencil, July 26, 2012

Haus 10, Passerelle / Building 10, aerial walkway
Foto / Photo: Georg Aerni

als ablesbares Skelett artikuliert. Sie wirken im Vergleich zu den grösseren Bauten eher wie Objekte und gewinnen dadurch einen noch höheren Grad an Abstraktion. In diesen massstäblich untergeordneten baulichen Situationen behandelt der Architekt die Stahlbauten als vermittelnde Elemente, die analog zu einem Möbel – oder gar einem Türgriff – eine Verbindung zwischen Betrachter und Haus artikulieren sollen.

ERSCHEINUNGSBILDER

Als Gestalt erzeugt das Haus 10 trotz seiner geometrisch einfachen Form einen rätselhaften Eindruck. Dies hat mit der Komplexität des heterogenen Umfelds zu tun, so wie auch mit der mehrdeutigen Erscheinung des Baukörpers. Selbst die Nutzung des Gebäudes ist auf den ersten Blick nicht sofort ablesbar. Und schliesslich erzeugt die andockende Passerelle ebenso wie die dicht angrenzende Hochgarage auf der Westseite den Eindruck, dass der Bau eng mit seiner Umgebung verwoben ist.

Wie eine Plastik entfaltet sich das Gebäude erst dann als komplexes Ganzes, wenn man es von allen Seiten betrachtet. Bewegt man sich von der oberen Hauptebene des Spitals um das Gebäude herum, vollführt man vereinfacht gesehen eine Spiralbewegung, die zum kinematischen Effekt des Objekts beiträgt. Betrachtet man das dunkelbraune Gebäude von Süden aus, wo die Verbindungsbrücke den Vordergrund dominiert, ruft es die Assoziation einer Burg hervor. Wenige Schritte weiter erinnert es – wegen seiner Ausrichtung parallel zum Hang sowie aufgrund der Verbindungsbrücke und des Schornsteins an der Westfassade – an einen im Hafen angedockten Ozeandampfer.

An der gegenüberliegenden Seite, von Norden aus, präsentiert sich das Haus eher wie ein kleines Bürogebäude. Die leicht schimmernde, vertikal gerippte Fassade, die an Cordsamt erinnert, erzeugt eine klassische moderne Anmutung, die den Bau als entfernten Verwandten der bronzenen Bürotürme eines Mies van der Rohe wirken lässt. Etwas gewagter könnte man aber auch meinen, es weise eine Verwandtschaft mit einigen von Hans Poelzigs Bauten und Entwürfen auf: konkret mit seinen Entwürfen für ein Bankgebäude in Dresden (1921) sowie das Verwaltungsgebäude der Gebrüder Meyer in Hannover (1923/24). In diesen beiden Entwürfen wird besonders das Verhältnis zwischen der einfachen Bauform und der Artikulation der Hülle thematisiert. Obwohl Poelzigs architektonische Sprache im Vergleich zu Fawad Kazi deutlich expressiver ist und es keine direkten Hinweise gibt, dass diese Bauten des deutschen Architekten als Vorbilder für das Spitalgebäude gedient haben, lassen sich

more like objects and thereby gain an even greater degree of abstraction. In this structural situation, secondary in terms of scale, the architect treats the steel structures as mediating elements, which — analogue to a piece of furniture, or even a door handle — are meant to articulate a connection between viewer and building.

APPEARANCES

Although its geometric form is simple, Building 10's impression as a shape is puzzling. This results from the complexity of the heterogenous environment and the building's complex appearance. At first glance, not even the use of the structure can be immediately deduced. And finally, the adjoining aerial walkway and directly adjacent multistory garage on the western side generate the impression that the building is tightly interwoven with its environment.

Similar to a sculpture, the building first develops to a complex whole when viewed from all sides. In simplified terms, moving around the building from the upper main level of the hospital occurs in a spiral movement, which adds to the structure's cinematic effect. Viewing the dark brown building from the south, where the foreground is dominated by the connecting bridge, associations with a castle arise. A few steps further — due to its orientation parallel to the slope, as well as the connecting bridge and smokestack on the western façade — it looks like an ocean liner docked in harbor.

On the opposite side, from the north, the building presents itself as more of a small office building. The slightly shimmering, vertically corrugated, corduroy-like façade generates a classical, modern impression, making the building appear to be a distant relative of a Mies van der Rohe bronze office tower. Going out on a limb, one could even say that it exhibits an affinity with several of Hans Poelzig's buildings and designs: specifically, with his design for a bank building in Dresden (1921) and the Gebrüder Meyer administrative building in Hanover (1923/24). These two designs focus especially on the relationship between a simple building form and the articulation of the shell. Although Poelzig's architectural language is clearly more expressive than Kazi's, and there is no direct evidence that these buildings by the German architect served as role models for the hospital building, similarities can be detected. Both architects employ a strongly articulated verticality and relief work on the building shell, which evokes a distinct textile effect. This adds an unexpected depth and complexity to the simple building volume. Furthermore, both

Hans Poelzig, Entwurf für ein Bankgebäude in Dresden, 1921 / Hans Poelzig, design for a bank building in Dresden, 1921

Haus 10, Nordwestfassade / Building 10, northwest façade
Foto / Photo: Georg Aerni

Ähnlichkeiten erkennen. Beide Architekten setzen eine stark artikulierte Vertikalität und Reliefierung der Gebäudehülle ein, was eine ausgeprägt textile Wirkung hervorruft. Dies fügt den einfachen Baukörpern eine unerwartete Tiefe und Komplexität hinzu. Weiters schaffen beide Architekten auf ähnliche Weise einen monumentalen Ausdruck, den nicht die Steigerung des Massstabs, sondern eher im feineren Register die subtile Arbeit an Proportion und Körperhaftigkeit erzeugt.

Aber die allerstärkste Assoziation, die das Haus 10 hervorruft – vor allem von Westen aus gesehen, wo der bereits erwähnte Schornstein im Zusammenspiel mit der Verbindungsbrücke die Bauform dominiert –, ist die eines Fabrikgebäudes. Das Bild der Fabrik als Motiv ist in der Architektur der Moderne tief verankert. Von Karl Friedrich Schinkels bekannten Skizzen von seiner Reise nach England im frühen 19. Jahrhundert, die als Leitbilder für seine spätere Architektur eine wesentliche Bedeutung hatten, bis zum Zelebrieren der Getreidesilos und amerikanischen Fabriken in Le Corbusiers Manifest *Vers une Architecture*[2] haben Industriebauten bis in die Gegenwart eine wichtige Rolle eingenommen und bilden das Fundament für die heutige Architektur – sowohl in konstruktiver als auch in ästhetischer Hinsicht. Der britische Theoretiker und Architekturhistoriker Reyner Banham hat in seinem Buch *Das gebaute Atlantis. Amerikanische Industriebauten und die frühe Moderne in Europa*[3] diese doppelte Auswirkung auf die Architektur ausführlich beschrieben.

Die Bildhaftigkeit und emotive Kraft von Industriearchitektur hat keiner so intensiv untersucht wie das deutsche Fotografenpaar Bernd und Hilla Becher. Über Jahrzehnte haben sie europäische und nordamerikanische Fabrikanlagen aufgesucht und systematisch in detailreichen, schattenlosen Bildern festgehalten. Von weiten Landschaftsaufnahmen bis zu Details haben ihre monumentalen Bilderserien eine fast hypnotisierende und zugleich melancholische Wirkung. Die abgebildeten Bauten erscheinen wie architektonische Urformen, die auf brachiale Weise zu einem komplexen Ganzen zusammengestellt werden, um ihre Zwecke für die Industrie zu erfüllen. Ein wichtiger Ordnungsbegriff im Werk von Bernd und Hilla Becher ist die «Typologie». Zahlreiche Serien von Wassertürmen, Silos, Hallen etc. spannen ein Bedeutungsfeld zwischen dem einzelnen Bauwerk und einem abstrakten Formenschema auf, das sich nur indirekt mit einer alltäglichen Architektur für Menschen in Verbindung setzen lässt. Ein zweites visuelles Ordnungsprinzip, das sie in ihrem fotografischen Werk einsetzen, ist die analytische Rotation um das Objekt herum, wie sie zum Beispiel in den Serien «Zeche Hannibal» und «Zeche Hannover»

architects achieve a monumental impression generated by subtle work on proportions and physicality in the fine details rather than through an increase in scale.

But the strongest association evoked by Building 10—especially when seen from the west, where the building form is dominated by the abovementioned smokestack in interplay with the connecting bridge—is that of a factory building. An image of the factory as motif is deeply anchored in modernist architecture. From Karl Friedrich Schinkel's famous sketches made during his travels in England in the early nineteenth century, which were crucial as models for his later architecture, through to Le Corbusier's celebration of the grain silos and American factories in his manifesto *Vers une Architecture*[2], industrial buildings have captured an important role through to the present, and form the foundation of today's architecture—in terms of both construction and aesthetics. The British theorist and achitectural historian Reyner Banham explained this double impact on architecture in great detail in *A Concrete Atlantis: U.S. Industrial Building and European Modern Architecture, 1900–1925.*[3]

The most intense investigation of the visual quality and emotive power of industrial architecture was carried out by the German photographers Bernd and Hilla Becher. They spent decades visiting European and North American factories and systematically capturing them in detailed, unshaded photos. From broad landscape shots through to details, their monumental photo series have a nearly hypnotizing and likewise melancholic effect. The depicted buildings look like architectural prototypes, which are brutally compiled as a complex whole to fulfill their industrial purpose. *Typology* is an important defining term in Bernd and Hilla Becher's oeuvre. Numerous series of water towers, silos, halls, etc., span a field of meaning between the individual buildings and an abstract scheme of shapes that can only indirectly be related to an everyday architecture for people. A second visual ordering principle that they employ in their photographic oeuvre is the analytical rotation around the object, which can be seen, for example, in the series "Coal Mine Hannibal" and "Coal Mine Hanover."[4] Here, individual parts of the production complexes, such as tower conveyor belts, transport paths, silos, and halls are illustrated frontally and at right angles from all sides. Despite the previously mentioned minimal geometry of the individual buildings, these series document an astoundingly great overall sculptural effect. Exactly this phenomenon can be observed in Building 10 of the Cantonal Hospital St.Gallen, as a result of implementation and topography.

Bernd und Hilla Becher, «Zeche Hannibal», 2000 / Bernd and Hilla Becher, "Coal Mine Hannibal" (Zeche Hannibal), 2000
Aus / From: *Bernd & Hilla Becher. Zeche Hannibal*, München: Schirmer/Mosel, 2000, S. 113

zu sehen ist.[4] Hier werden einzelne Teile der Produktionsanlagen wie Turmförderanlagen, Landabsätze, Silos und Hallen frontal und übereck von allen Seiten abgebildet. Diese Serien dokumentieren trotz der oben genannten reduzierten Geometrie des einzelnen Gebäudes eine verblüffend hohe plastische Gesamtwirkung. Es ist genau dieses Phänomen, das sich beim Haus 10 des Kantonsspitals St.Gallen als Folge von Setzung und Topografie beobachten lässt.

SILHOUETTE

Konkret ist der besagte Rauchfang ein Hinweis, dass das Haus 10 nicht nur Räume für Behandlung und Pflege beherbergt, sondern hier auch die Notstromgeneratoren für das gesamte Krankenhaus untergebracht sind. In einer zweigeschossigen Halle, die gefühlt die Hälfte des Erdgeschosses einnimmt, befinden sich drei imposante, gelb lackierte Dieselmotoren, die im Fall eines Stromausfalls das ganze Spital mit Energie versorgen können. Der Halle ist ein Schacht bzw. Vorbau an der Westfassade angefügt, der sich von aussen als eine Abstufung der Gebäudesilhouette abzeichnet. Dieser Bauteil ist mit grossen Lüftungslamellen versehen und speist die sauerstoffhungrigen Brennmotoren mit frischer Luft. Der erzeugte Rauch wiederum wird über den in die Fassade integrierten Rauchfang abgestossen. Wie im Pavillonbau wird auch hier aus einer technischen Notwendigkeit eine Tugend gemacht, und der Schornstein trägt somit massgeblich zum Gesamtausdruck des Gebäudes bei. Einige der oben aufgezählten Bildassoziationen würden ohne die präzise Artikulation dieser Silhouette nicht entstehen.

ANKOMMEN

Im täglichen Gebrauch ist das sechsgeschossige Gebäude – wie bereits erwähnt – über die Passerelle von der Südseite erschlossen. Das Personal und die Patiententransporte kommen im dritten Obergeschoss an, während die Öffentlichkeit das Gebäude im Geschoss darüber, im vierten Obergeschoss, betritt. Aber der eigentliche, strassenseitige Haupteingang befindet sich auf der Nordseite des Gebäudes und ist der Umgebung an der Steinachstrasse zugewandt. Dadurch bildet das Haus 10 ein Gelenk zwischen dem nördlichen Umfeld und dem Spitalareal – von dem aus man mit dem Lift hinauf zur Passerelle fahren kann und sich anschliessend auf dem Hauptniveau des Spitals weiterbewegt. Von aussen betrachtet ist der einfache Betonrahmen, der den Eingang markiert, verhältnismässig bescheiden, und er steht im Einklang mit der pragmatischen Funktion des Hauses. Es handelt sich in erster Linie um ein utilitaristisches Gebäude ohne

SILHOUETTE

The previously mentioned chimney clearly indicates that Building 10 not only provides spaces for treatment and care but also stores emergency electrical generators for the entire hospital. In a two-story hall, which takes up what seems like half of the ground floor, are three impressive, yellow-painted diesel motors that are able to supply the entire hospital with energy in the event of a power failure. In front of the hall is a shaft or porch on the west façade, which from outside stands out as a gradation of the building's silhouette. This part of the building is furnished with large ventilation lamella and feeds fresh air to the oxygen-starved combustion engines. The smoke generated is, in turn, released via the chimney integrated into the façade. Like in the pavilion building, here, too, a technical necessity becomes a virtue, and the chimney thus makes a crucial contribution to the overall expression of the building. Without the precise articulation of this silhouette, several of the previously mentioned visual associations would not have come about.

ARRIVAL

In daily use, the six-story building—as already mentioned—is accessed from the southern side via the aerial walkway. Staff and transported patients arrive on the third floor while the public enters the building on the floor above, on the fourth floor. But the actual, street-facing main entrance is on the northern side of the building and is turned toward the surroundings on Steinachstrasse. Building 10 thereby forms a link between the northern surroundings and the hospital grounds—one can travel from there by elevator to the aerial walkway and then continue onward at the main level of the hospital. Viewed from outside, the simple concrete framework that marks the entry is relatively modest and in line with the building's pragmatic function. It is, first and foremost, a utilitarian building with no major gestures. This reflects a general trend that can likewise be seen in the context of the new institutional buildings in St.Gallen mentioned at the start. All of these buildings exhibit relatively modest entry situations that are subordinate to the granularity of their façades—monumentality is dispensed with. Larger representative halls first develop inside in some of the buildings.

This applies only indirectly to Building 10 as here there is no spatial exaltation of the space. The entry area's representative effect occurs instead by means of high-class materialization. The floor is thus made of an extremely beautifully polished concrete typical in the region, with visible aggregate running through all of

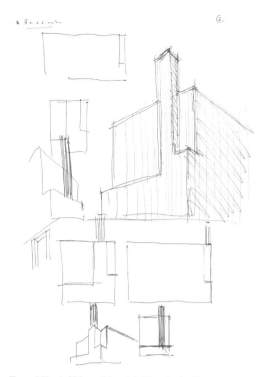

Fawad Kazi, Skizzenblatt A4, Kugelschreiber, 10.11.2014 / Fawad Kazi, A4 sketch, pen, November 10, 2014

grosse Gesten. Im Zusammenhang mit den oben genannten institutionellen St. Galler Neubauten zeichnet sich in diesem Punkt ebenfalls eine allgemeine Tendenz ab. Diese Gebäude weisen alle verhältnismässig bescheidene Eingangssituationen auf, die sich der Körnung ihrer Fassaden unterordnen – man verzichtet auf Monumentalität. Erst im Inneren entfalten sich teilweise grössere repräsentative Hallen.

Beim Haus 10 trifft dies nur indirekt zu. Hier wird nicht mit einer räumlichen Überhöhung des Raums gearbeitet. Die repräsentative Wirkung des Eingangsbereichs ergibt sich stattdessen aus einer hochwertigeren Materialisierung. So besteht der Boden aus einem sehr schön geschliffenen, ortsüblichen Beton mit sichtbarem Zuschlag, der sich durch alle Liftlobbys und das öffentlich zugängliche Treppenhaus zieht. Als Pendant zu dieser eleganten Bodenoberfläche wirkt eine kassettierte Decke mit klassischen Spiegelkopflampen. Dieses raffinierte Gestaltungselement erinnert auf den ersten Blick an die ikonische Decke über dem Eingang des Hauses von Adolf Loos am Michaelerplatz in Wien. Aber Kazi nennt hier als Referenz ein anderes Wiener Vorbild, nämlich das Funkhaus von Clemens Holzmeister. Bei näherer Betrachtung fällt auf, dass nicht nur die Ausführung der Beleuchtung im Haus 10 Parallelen zu dem für Wien aussergewöhnlichen Gebäude aufweist. Die formale Komplexität, die erst auf den zweiten Blick sichtbar wird, die rigorose Raumstruktur sowie das Alternieren zwischen Feierlichkeit und Strenge sind Merkmale, die auf beide Bauten zutreffen und die sie von der verspielteren Architektur eines Adolf Loos unterscheiden.

Dieses ungerichtete Feld von Lichtern komplettiert ein linearer Gegensatz in den Gangbereichen. Ein seitlich an der Decke positionierter Lichtstreifen beleuchtet die Erschliessungswege, damit den Patientinnen und Patienten in ihren Betten das Licht nicht direkt in die Augen scheint.

STRUKTUR

Im Sockelbereich des zukünftigen Neubaus (Haus 07A, 07B und OKS) wird für die Behandlungsstationen eine Geschosshöhe von 4.42 Metern geplant, während die Bettentürme mit 3.40 Metern auskommen. Das Haus 10 ist hingegen als Alleskönner konzipiert und soll sowohl Behandlungsstationen als auch Bettenplätze aufnehmen können. Das hat dazu geführt, dass Fawad Kazi für dieses Haus den exakten Mittelwert zwischen den beiden Raumhöhen gewählt hat, nämlich 3.91 Meter (4.42 + 3.40 Meter / 2). Nur das oberste Geschoss weist eine grössere Raumhöhe auf.

the elevator lobbies and the publicly accessible stairway. A coffered ceiling with classical head mirror bulbs offers a counterpart to this elegant floor surface. At first glance, this sophisticated design element recalls the iconic ceiling over the entrance to Adolf Loos's building on Vienna's Michaelerplatz. However, here Kazi is quoting a different role model from Vienna, namely, the Funkhaus broadcasting center by Clemens Holzmeister. Upon closer inspection it is obvious that there are more parallels between Building 10 and Holzmeister's building than the realization of the lighting, which, for its part, is exceptional for Vienna. First becoming visible on second glance are a formal complexity, rigorous spatial structure, and an alternation between festivity and severity, features of both buildings that distinguish them from Loos's more playful architecture.

This undirected field of lights completes a linear contrast in the hallway areas. A strip of lights positioned sideways on the ceiling illuminates the accessways so as not to shine directly into the eyes of the patients in their beds.

STRUCTURE

A floor level of 4.42 meters is planned for the treatment stations in the base area of the future new buildings (Buildings 07A, 07B, and OKS), while the inpatient towers will have room heights of 3.40 meters. Building 10, on the contrary, is conceived as an all-rounder and can absorb both treatment stations as well as inpatient wards. This led Kazi to choose the exact average of the two floor levels for this building, namely, 3.91 meters (4.42 + 3.40 meters / 2). Only the uppermost floor presents an exception and has a greater room height.

The building is a simple reinforced concrete skeleton structure with an axis dimension of 8.10 × 8.10 meters, analogous to the main buildings mentioned. Similar to a classical office building, the support structure is braced by two elongated cores poured on-site. Lengthwise, the volume is divided into two layers: facing the valley and oriented northward are the treatment rooms, while turned toward the south and the slope are the service area and vertical access cores. Finally, office spaces, which extend across the entire depth of the volume, can be accommodated on both ends of the longish building.

The southward-lying cores, which together with the inserted entry hall make up the building's permanent areas, complete the adaptable spatial structure. Entry hall, lift lobby, and main stairway also spatially shape a coherent unit, which is emphasized by the continuous materiality of the polished concrete. At the same time,

Clemens Holzmeister (nach Plänen von Heinrich Schmid und Hermann Aichinger), Funkhaus Wien, Wien, 1935–1939 / Clemens Holzmeister (based on plans by Heinrich Schmid and Hermann Aichinger), Funkhaus Wien, Vienna, 1935–1939
Foto / Photo: Hertha Hurnaus

Haus 10, Eingangshalle / Building 10, entrance hall
Foto / Photo: Georg Aerni

Das Gebäude ist ein einfacher Stahlbeton-Skelettbau mit einem Achsmass von 8.10 × 8.10 Metern, analog zu den oben aufgeführten Hauptbauten. Wie ein klassisches Bürogebäude wird das Traggerüst von zwei vor Ort betonierten, länglichen Kernen ausgesteift. In Längsrichtung ist das Gebäude in zwei Schichten geteilt: Talseitig und gegen Norden ausgerichtet befinden sich die Behandlungsräume, während die Servicebereiche und vertikalen Erschliessungskerne nach Süden dem Hang zugewandt sind. Schliesslich lassen sich grössere Buroräume, die sich über die volle Tiefe des Gebäudes erstrecken, an den Stirnseiten des Gebäudes unterbringen.

Die südseitig gelegenen Kerne, die zusammen mit der durchgesteckten Eingangshalle die permanenten Bereiche des Gebäudes ausmachen, komplettieren die adaptierbare Raumstruktur. Eingangshalle, Liftlobby und Haupttreppe bilden auch räumlich gesehen eine zusammenhängende Einheit, was die durchgehende Materialität des geschliffenen Betons hervorhebt. Gleichzeitig stehen Treppenhaus und Lobby auch in einem räumlichen Spannungsverhältnis. Die oben erwähnte Deckenbeleuchtung taucht die Betonoberflächen, Holzfensterrahmen und Liftportale aus Edelstahl in ein sanftes, warmes Licht, das eine feierliche Atmosphäre erzeugt. Unerwartet edel für ein Spitalgebäude vermittelt der Treppenraum hingegen eine kontemplative, beinahe sakrale Atmosphäre, akzentuiert von punktuellen Ausblicken. Als Kontrast ist das Kunstlicht hier als durchgehender Lichtstreifen in den wuchtigen, aber dennoch elegant wirkenden Handlauf aus Eiche eingelassen. Diese indirekte Beleuchtung unterstützt das Raumgefühl dieses Erschliessungselements, das hoffentlich dazu beitragen kann, dass die Treppen im Alltag häufiger als üblicherweise benutzt werden.

Die Bauweise der Aussenwand ist für den Skelettbau bekanntlich eine der Hauptfragen. Von der Anwendung des Prüssbzw. Kessler-Wandsystems bei Poelzig[5] bis zu den I-Trägern in den Turmbauten eines Mies van der Rohe entfaltet sich hier ein umfassendes Spektrum von baugeschichtlichen Lösungen. Am häufigsten kommt aber eine gemauerte Wandausfachung zur Anwendung, die entweder verputzt oder mit Sichtbacksteinen versehen wird bzw. mit einer anderen Art von vorgehängter Fassadenhülle.

Auch das Haus 10 folgt dem letzten Prinzip. Aber anstelle einer vor Ort gemauerten Innenschale wurden für dieses Bauwerk raumhohe Betonfertigteile mit einer Wandstärke von 14 Zentimetern eingesetzt. Auf den ersten Blick könnte dadurch der Eindruck einer konstruktiven Redundanz entstehen – es wäre leicht the stairway and lobby are also in a charged spatial relationship. The previously mentioned ceiling lighting submerges the concrete surfaces, wooden window frames, and stainless-steel elevator doors in a smooth, warm light that generates a festive atmosphere. On the other hand, the stairway, unexpectedly noble for a hospital, mediates a contemplative, nearly sacral mood accentuated by sporadic views. In contrast, artificial light is embedded as a continuous bar of light in the massive but nonetheless elegant oak handrail. The indirect lighting supports the spatial atmosphere of this access element, which will hopefully contribute to the stairs being used in daily life more frequently than usual.

The architecture of the exterior walls is clearly one of the main issues in a skeleton structure. From Poelzig's application of Prüss or Kessler wall systems[5] through to the I-beams in Mies van der Rohe's tower buildings, architectural history reveals a broad spectrum of solutions. Most frequently employed, however, is a masoned wall bracing, which is either plastered or furnished with exposed bricks, or another type of prehung façade shell.

Building 10, too, follows the latter principle. However, rather than an inner shell built on-site, here, a floor-to-ceiling prefabricated concrete section with a 14-centimeter thick-wall is inserted. At first glance, it may seem as though this is a structural redundancy—it would be easy to imagine that these wall panels, with a few additional centimeters of wall depth, could serve as supporting elements, thus making the supports structurally redundant. However, as explained, a skeleton structure always requires an additional wall between its main supports, and the same structural "redundancy" appears also with a brick masonry wall. The architect's argument for choosing this building method is based on the greater precision that can be achieved in the factory. In this way, a more precise window alignment can be produced and the untreated concrete can be left exposed in the interior. As compared with a lightweight construction or masoned exterior wall including the associated work steps, it is entirely plausible to speak of an optimization of costs and corresponding aesthetic added value.

SYSTEMATIC OF SURFACES
All windows are realized as conventional wood-aluminum frames, whereby the inside spruce wood remains natural. They are additionally equipped with white curtains to provide privacy. This materialization, which is unusual for an institutional building, contributes greatly to the pleasant, comfortable feeling of the interior spaces—a welcome quality for a hospital.

Ludwig Mies van der Rohe, Seagram Building, New York, 1954–1958
Foto / Photo: Nicolai Schneider

18

vorstellbar, dass diese Wandpaneele mit ein paar Zentimetern zusätzlicher Wandstärke als tragende Elemente dienen könnten und die Stützen dadurch konstruktiv überflüssig würden. Aber wie gesagt verlangt der Skelettbau in jedem Fall eine zusätzliche Aussenwand zwischen den Hauptstützen, und die gleiche konstruktive «Redundanz» trifft auch bei einer gemauerten Backsteinwand zu. Seitens des Architekten wird für die gewählte Bauweise mit der grösseren Präzision argumentiert, die sich werkseitig erreichen lässt. Dadurch lassen sich die Fensteranschlüsse genauer herstellen und ausserdem kann die Innenseite aus unbehandeltem Beton roh belassen werden. Im Vergleich zu einer Aussenwand in Leichtbauweise oder einem Mauerwerk und den damit verbundenen Arbeitsschritten ist es somit durchaus plausibel, von einer Optimierung der Kosten mit entsprechendem ästhetischen Mehrwert zu sprechen.

SYSTEMATIK DER OBERFLÄCHEN

Alle Fenster sind als konventionelle Holz-Aluminium-Rahmen ausgeführt, wobei das innenseitige Fichtenholz naturbelassen bleibt. Zusätzlich sind sie mit weissen Vorhängen versehen, die als Sichtschutz dienen. Diese für ein institutionelles Gebäude unübliche Materialisierung trägt viel dazu bei, dass die Innenräume angenehm wohnlich wirken – für ein Krankenhaus eine willkommene Qualität.

Das Weglassen eines Farbanstrichs auf den Fensterrahmen lässt sich über die Raumwirkung hinaus auch auf eine allgemeine Systematik der Farbgebung zurückführen: Der Architekt strebte in erster Linie die Eigenfarben des Materials an. Dies betrifft vor allem die bereits erwähnten Beton-, Edelstahl- und Holzoberflächen. Als zweite Ebene werden Beläge wie Linoleum und Fliesen, zusammen mit Vorhängen und Möbeln in naturnahen Farben ausgeführt, die sich im Farbspektrum des Betonzuschlags wiederfinden lassen (z. B. Grün, Braun, Violett, Beige). Eine besondere Kategorie bilden die Türen. Die Farben der Zargen und Türblätter sind in drei unterschiedlichen Grautönen ausgeführt, jeweils in Abhängigkeit von den Wänden, in denen sie sitzen, bzw. von den Funktionen, die sie erschliessen. Ausserdem wird mit zwei Typen von Einbaumöbeln eine lesbare Differenzierung zwischen den Empfangsbereichen (Eichenholzfurnier) und Behandlungsstationen (Kunstharz) erzeugt. Zusätzliche, nicht bauliche Farbakzente liefern das Mobiliar, wie etwa der ikonische Schalensessel von Ray und Charles Eames, sowie eine beeindruckende Zahl von gerahmten Grafiken des Künstlers Jean-Christophe de Clercq. Überhaupt spielt die Kunst auch für das übergeordnete

The omission of a coat of paint on the window frames can also be traced back beyond the spatial effect to a general systematic approach to coloring: the architect sought primarily the materials' own colors. This applies mainly to the already mentioned concrete, stainless steel, and wood surfaces. As a second level, coatings such as linoleum and tiles, along with curtains and furniture, are in naturalistic colors, which can be found again in the color spectrum of the concrete aggregate (for example, green, brown, violet, beige). The doors comprise a special category. The colors of the frames and door leaves are realized in three different shades of gray, each depending on the walls in which they are located or the functions that they access. Apart from that, two types of built-in furniture generate a legible differentiation between the entry areas (oak veneer) and treatment stations (synthetic resin). Additional, nonstructural color accents are provided by the furniture, such as the iconic shell chairs by Ray and Charles Eames, as well as an impressive number of framed prints by the artist Jean-Christophe de Clercq. Art plays an important role also for the overriding hospital expansion project in general. It is clearly recognizable that the client views the visual quality of the premises as an integrative element of treatment.

Some of the workspaces are set up in group offices. These spaces exhibit an airy, bright atmosphere beyond the spatial economy, with a distant view to the surroundings, which would come far less into play in a cellular structure. At the same time, the spaces achieve a measure of intimacy and comfort through the green carpeting and textile table niches, which support the staff's focused work. Apart from that, glazed meeting cubicles offer an additional acoustic boundary for small meetings.

ATMOSPHERE

In today's architectural discourse, the concepts of atmosphere and the associated spatial phenomenology are central themes. They are ascribed a mediating function between the built world and the psychology of the user. How a structure affects people within the building at an emotional level, is therewith considered a key issue in today's architectural discourse.[6] For that reason, it is remarkable that Kazi hardly speaks about the atmospheric impact of his architecture—although his structures, as already described, are distinctly atmospheric and offer experiential value. Instead, Kazi argues from a structural and programmatic point of view. He sees architecture as an intellectual achievement, which develops from an inner regularity and does not primarily pursue the goal of generating an atmosphere or an image. For Kazi, the fact that

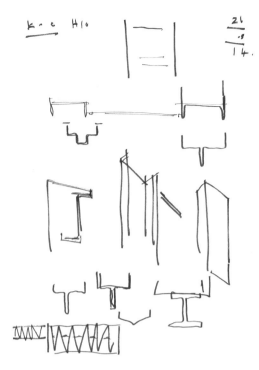

Fawad Kazi, Skizzenblatt A4, Filzstift, 26.08.2014/ Fawad Kazi, A4 sketch, felt pen, August 26, 2014

Spitalerweiterungsprojekt eine wichtige Rolle. Es ist eindeutig erkennbar, dass die Bauherrschaft die visuelle Qualität der Räumlichkeiten als integratives Element der Behandlung betrachtet.

Ein Teil der Arbeitsplätze ist in Gruppenbüros eingerichtet. Diese Räume weisen jenseits der Flächenökonomie eine luftig-helle Atmosphäre mit weiten Blicken über die Umgebung auf, was in einer zellularen Struktur deutlich weniger zum Tragen käme. Gleichzeitig erreichen die Räume aber dank des grünen Teppichbodens und der textilen Tischnischen ein Mass an Intimität und Geborgenheit, das die konzentrierte Arbeit des Personals unterstützt. Für kleine Besprechungen bieten verglaste Besprechungskabinen ausserdem eine zusätzliche akustische Abgrenzung.

ATMOSPHÄRE

Im heutigen Architekturdiskurs sind die Begriffe der Atmosphäre und der damit verbundenen Raumphänomenologie zentrale Themen. Ihnen wird eine vermittelnde Funktion zwischen der gebauten Welt und der Psychologie der Nutzer zugeschrieben. Wie ein Bau auf einer emotionalen Ebene auf die Menschen im Gebäude wirkt, wird somit als eine zentrale Frage des heutigen Architekturdiskurses gesehen.[6] Es ist daher auffallend, dass Fawad Kazi – obwohl seine Bauten wie bereits beschrieben eindeutig stimmungsvoll sind und einen Erlebniswert bieten – kaum über die atmosphärische Wirkung seiner Architektur spricht. Vielmehr argumentiert Kazi aus einer konstruktiven und programmatischen Sicht. Er sieht Architektur als eine intellektuelle Leistung, die sich aus einer inneren Gesetzmässigkeit heraus entwickelt und nicht vorrangig das Ziel verfolgt, eine Atmosphäre oder ein Bild zu erzeugen. Dass sie nichtsdestotrotz zu wirkungsvollen, atmosphärischen Bauwerken führt, stellt sich für Kazi indes nicht als Widerspruch dar, sondern als Konsequenz. Diese Haltung lässt sich zu derjenigen des Wiener Altmeisters Hermann Czech in Bezug stellen. Unlängst artikulierte Czech in einem Interview mit dem deutschen Architekturtheoretiker Tom Schoper unter dem Titel «Von Dingen, die nach nichts ausschauen» seine Ablehnung von «Atmosphäre» als leistungsfähigem Begriff in der Architektur:

«Hier tappt man nun aber ausdrücklich in die Falle, Architektur auf ihren Erlebniswert zu reduzieren und diesen als ein Verkaufs- oder als ein Werbeargument zu verwenden – eben weil Architektur hier ausschließlich von der Konsumtion, vom Konsumenten her gedacht wird. [...] In meiner Sichtweise stehen Produzent und Konsument einander gegenüber. In der ausschließlichen Sichtweise des Erlebnisses der Konsumtion betrachte ich this nevertheless leads to an effective, atmospheric architecture is a consequence, not a contradiction. This attitude can be seen in relation to that of the Viennese *Altmeister* Hermann Czech. In a recent interview with the German architectural theorist Tom Schoper, entitled "Von Dingen, die nach nichts ausschauen" (On things that don't look like much), Czech articulated his rejection of "atmosphere" as an efficient concept in architecture:

"But here, one falls explicitly into the trap of reducing architecture to its experiential value, and using this as a sales or advertising argument—precisely because here, architecture is thought of exclusively in terms of consumption, for consumers. [...] In my way of looking at it, producer and consumer oppose one another. In the exclusive perspective of the experience of consumption, I consider a work under the aspect: do I like it or not? But you don't 'understand' a work as product. You truly understand it only when you empathize with the line of thought of production, when you try to comprehend its motivation, try to understand the mode of the formation process. That first leads to an understanding of art. Only then do you enter into dialogue with the work. But when you begin simply from an 'aesthetic' impression, along consumptive lines, you remain 'left out.'"[7]

On the contrary, the concept of production takes a central role in Hermann Czech's design process: "I understand production as production of architectural thoughts, not as production in the sense of building and making."[8] This understanding of architecture as an intellectual endeavor concerned with the roots of architectural problems can also be transferred to Kazi's design work. As for Czech, this attitude does not at all mean negation of design issues in the sense of composing—quite the contrary, it is possible to claim that both architects pursue form and creating form as the primary goals of architectural production.

SYNTHESIS

Fawad Kazi's oeuvre is characterized by sophisticated constructions that have emerged from a patient and prolonged process. The individual buildings are part of a continuous grappling with the same motif: the poetic power of structural logics. Referring to the statement by Hermann Czech that architecture is, first and foremost, the product of a thought process, Kazi's architecture, too, can be designated as built idea. Just as an equation can have an aesthetic value for a mathematician, Kazi aspires toward logically beautiful architectural solutions with his projects. At issue is structural regularity and about how building elements can be assembled in a compelling way.

Hermann Czech, Restaurant Salzamt, Wien / Vienna, 1983
Foto / Photo: Margherita Spiluttini

Haus 10, 4. Obergeschoss, Anmelde- und Wartebereich Onkologie/Hämatologie / Building 10, 4th floor, registration and waiting area oncology/hematology
Foto / Photo: Georg Aerni

ein Werk unter dem Aspekt: gefällt es mir oder gefällt es mir nicht? So ‹versteht› man ein Werk aber nicht als Produkt. Wirklich verstehen kann man es erst, wenn man sich in den Gedankengang der Produktion hineinversetzt, wenn man seine Motivation nachzuvollziehen versucht, wenn man sich in den Modus des Entstehungsprozesses hineindenkt. Das erst führt zum Verstehen von Kunst. Dann erst kommt man in ein Gespräch mit dem Werk. Wenn man nur von einer ‹ästhetischen› Anmutung ausgeht, im konsumtiven Sinn gedacht, bleibt man ‹außen vor›.»[7] Hingegen nimmt der Begriff Produktion in Hermann Czechs Entwurfsarbeit eine zentrale Stelle ein: «Produktion verstehe ich als Produktion architektonischer Gedanken, nicht als Produktion im Sinne des Bauens und des Machens.»[8] Dieses Verständnis von Architektur als eine intellektuelle Arbeit, die sich mit den Wurzeln architektonischer Fragestellungen befasst, lässt sich auch auf die Entwurfsarbeit von Fawad Kazi übertragen. Wie bei Hermann Czech bedeutet diese Haltung hingegen noch lange nicht, dass Gestaltungsfragen im Sinne des Komponierens negiert werden – im Gegenteil lässt sich behaupten, dass beide Architekten Form und Formgebung als primäre Ziele der architektonischen Produktion verfolgen.

SYNTHESE
Fawad Kazis Werk kennzeichnen raffinierte Bauten, die aus einem geduldigen und langwierigen Prozess hervorgegangen sind. Die einzelnen Gebäude sind Teil einer kontinuierlichen Auseinandersetzung mit dem gleichen Motiv: der poetischen Kraft einer konstruktiven Logik. In Anlehnung an die oben erwähnte Aussage von Hermann Czech, dass Architektur in erster Linie das Produkt eines Gedankenprozesses sei, kann auch Kazis Architektur als gebaute Idee bezeichnet werden. Wie eine Gleichung für einen Mathematiker einen ästhetischen Wert haben kann, strebt Kazi mit seinen Projekten logisch schöne architektonische Lösungen an. Es handelt sich um konstruktive Gesetzmässigkeiten und darum, wie sich Bauteile auf schlüssige Weise zusammenfügen lassen.

Seine bisherigen Bauten können übergeordnet betrachtet als architektonische Studien verstanden werden, die als Hauptmotiv jeweils eine spezifische, für die Aufgabe relevante Fragestellung verfolgen. Bei der Erweiterung der Schulanlage Fagen in Bozen (2001–2009) stand zum Beispiel das Einschneiden von Fensteröffnungen in einen prismatischen Betonkörper im Vordergrund. In diesem Frühwerk ist ausserdem eine Affinität zur Architektursprache des Wiener Architekten Adolf Krischanitz feststellbar, bei dem Kazi eine Zeit lang gearbeitet hat, bevor er

Kazi's hitherto structures, viewed from a macro level, can be understood as architectural studies, which each pursue, as a main motif, a specific problem relevant for the task. With the expansion of the Fagen School Center in Bolzano (2001–2009), for example, at the forefront was the cutting of window openings into a prismatic concrete volume. Moreover, detectable in this early work is an affinity to the architectural language of the Viennese architect Adolf Krischanitz, whom Kazi worked together with for a time before founding his own office. The subsequent ETH LEE building in Zurich (2007–2015) can be summarized simply as a study in subtle differentiation—from the building's memorable silhouette through to the delicate molding of the prefabricated façade. This project also had a direct reference: the relationship to design themes from Hans Kollhoff's architectural language. Kollhoff, Kazi's former professor at the ETH, was extremely important in his understanding of architecture.[9] It is interesting to observe how these two reference figures, viewed in a simplified way, represent two opposing perceptions of architecture—one abstract (Krischanitz) and one structurally concrete, emphasizing the tectonic (Kollhoff). Kazi's works hitherto unfold between these two poles in the spectrum of architectural expression. But Building 10 points beyond this duality and stands out as a synthesis of the two architectures.

REFERENCE BUILDING
As mentioned several times, Kazi sees Building 10 as a prototype for the large hospital buildings to come. Even when it might go too far to speak of a sketch along the lines of a maquette in sculpture, this indirect connection between model and final result leads to a special tension for Building 10. The building obviously does not stand for itself alone, like Kazi's earlier structures. The aspect of "study" also does not apply here in the same way. Building 10 instead tells an independent, complex story and forms the nucleus for a significantly larger structure. The story is one of an intriguing architecture—a simple basic form which raises numerous associations. The spatial structure is also clear and organized and exhibits no unnecessary complexity. But in its overlapping of the permanent basic framework and configuration of the access figure through to materialization, the building generates a complex form, also inside. In other words, it is a convincing example of an architecture that, at many levels, generates a calm complexity and spatial wealth. Building 10 represents an attitude to design that yields an abstract but at the same time humane architecture that is capable of standing the test as a

1 Gottfried Semper, *Der Stil in den technischen und tektonischen Künsten oder praktische Ästhetik: ein Handbuch für Techniker, Künstler und Kunstfreunde,* Band 1: *Die textile Kunst für sich betrachtet und in Beziehung zur Baukunst,* Frankfurt/Main 1860, https://digi.ub.uni-heidelberg.de/diglit/semper1860
2 Le Corbusier, *Vers une architecture,* Paris 1923
3 Reyner Banham, *Das gebaute Atlantis. Amerikanische Industriebauten und die frühe Moderne in Europa,* Basel 1990
4 Bernd und Hilla Becher, *Zeche Hannibal,* München 2000 und *Zeche Hannover,* München 2010
5 Franz Hart, «Zur Geschichte des Backsteinbaus», in: *Werk, Bauen + Wohnen* 09/1981, S. 10–15, hier S. 14, http://doi.org/10.5169/seals-51979 (abgerufen am 05.06.2019): «Der Leitgedanke des Entwurfs ist der Kontrast zwischen einer Skelettbauweise für die Fabrikationsräume – die ‹Kesslerwand›, eine Art Eisenfachwerk aus hochkantgestellten Ziegeln – und den massiv ausgeführten Bauteilen für die Sozialräume und Treppenhäuser.» Siehe auch Erich Mindner, *Wände und Decken,* Band I *Wände,* Berlin 1936, S. 128–131
6 Siehe unter anderem: Peter Zumthor, *Atmosphären,* Basel 2006 und Gernot Böhme, *Architektur und Atmosphäre,* München 2006
7 Tom Schoper, «Von Dingen, die nach nichts ausschauen. Ein Gespräch mit Hermann Czech, Wien», in: Tom Schoper, *Ein Haus. Werk – Ding – Zeug?,* 2. Aufl., Wien 2017, S. 56 und 58
8 Ibid, S. 59
9 David Ganzoni, «Die Lehre Kollhoffs. Von der Grossform zur Fassade. 25 Jahre lehrte Hans Kollhoff Architektur an der ETH Zürich. Über die Nachwirkungen in der Schweizer Architektur», in: *Hochparterre* 24, 11/2011, S. 22f.

sein eigenes Büro gründete. Das darauffolgende ETH LEE-Gebäude in Zürich (2007–2015) kann einfach zusammengefasst als eine Studie in subtiler Differenzierung verstanden werden – von der einprägsamen Gebäudesilhouette bis zur feingliedrigen Formung der Fertigteilfassade. Auch dieses Projekt hat einen direkten referenziellen Bezug: die Verwandtschaft zu gestalterischen Themen aus Hans Kollhoffs Architektursprache. Als sein einstiger Professor an der ETH hat Kollhoff eine grosse Bedeutung für Kazis Architekturverständnis.[9] Es ist interessant zu beobachten, wie diese beiden «Bezugspersonen», vereinfacht betrachtet, zwei gegensätzliche Architekturempfindungen vertreten – eine abstrakte (Krischanitz) und eine konstruktiv-konkrete, die das Tektonische betont (Kollhoff). Die bisherigen Arbeiten von Fawad Kazi entfalten sich zwischen diesen beiden Polen eines architektonischen Sprachspektrums. Aber das Haus 10 weist über diese Dualität hinaus und zeichnet sich als Synthese der beiden Architekturen ab.

REFERENZBAU

Wie mehrfach erwähnt, sieht Fawad Kazi das Haus 10 als Prototyp für die kommenden grossen Spitalbauten. Auch wenn es vielleicht zu weit gehen würde, von einer Skizze im Sinne einer Maquette in der Bildhauerei zu sprechen, führt diese indirekte Verbindung zwischen Modell und Endergebnis zu einer besonderen Spannung für das Haus 10. Das Gebäude steht offensichtlich nicht wie Kazis frühere Bauten für sich allein. Auch der Aspekt der «Studie» ist hier nicht auf die gleiche Weise zutreffend. Das Haus 10 erzählt eher eine eigenständige, komplexe Geschichte, und es bildet die Keimzelle für eine deutlich grössere Struktur. Die «Geschichte» ist die einer spannungsvollen Architektur – eine einfache Grundform, die zahlreiche Assoziationen hervorruft. Auch die Raumstruktur ist klar und geordnet und weist keine unnötige Komplexität auf. Aber in seiner Überlagerung des permanenten Grundgerüsts sowie der Konfiguration der Erschliessungsfigur bis hin zur Materialisierung erzeugt das Gebäude auch im Inneren ein komplexes Gebilde. Es ist mit anderen Worten ein überzeugendes Beispiel für eine Architektur, die auf vielen Ebenen eine unaufgeregte Komplexität und räumlichen Reichtum erzeugt. Das Haus 10 steht für eine Entwurfshaltung, die eine abstrakte, aber zugleich humane Architektur hervorbringt, die imstande ist, sich im Wirrwarr der heutigen Stadtstruktur als Zufluchtsort und Orientierungspunkt zu bewähren. Für ein Spitalgebäude könnte man sich nicht mehr wünschen.

place of refuge and site of orientation in the confusing tangle of today's urban structure. For a hospital building, one couldn't wish for anything more.

1   Gottfried Semper, *Style in the Technical and Tectonic Arts, Or, Practical Aesthetics*, ed. Harry Francis Malgrave, trans. Michael Robinson (Los Angeles, 2004).
2   Le Corbusier, *Vers une architecture* (Paris, 1923); translated as *Toward an Architecture* (Los Angeles, 2007).
3   Reyner Banham, *A Concrete Atlantis: U.S. Industrial Building and European Modern Architecture*, 1900–1925 (Cambridge, MA, 1989).
4   Bernd and Hilla Becher, *Zeche Hannibal* (Munich, 2000) and *Zeche Hannover* (Munich, 2010).
5   Franz Hart, "Zur Geschichte des Backsteinbaus," *Werk, Bauen + Wohnen*, no. 9 (1981), 10–15, here 14, http://doi.org/10.5169/seals-51979 (accessed June 5, 2019): "The guiding concept for the design is the contrast between a skeleton building method for the production spaces—the 'Kesslerwand,' a type of iron truss of upright placed bricks—and the solid-built building parts for the social spaces and stairway." See also Erich Mindner, *Wände und Decken*, vol. 1, *Wände* (Berlin, 1936), 128–131.
6   See, among others: Peter Zumthor, *Atmospheres: Architectural Environments. Surrounding Objects* (Basel, 2006) and Gernot Böhme, *Architektur und Atmosphäre* (Munich, 2006).
7   Tom Schoper, "Von Dingen, die nach nichts ausschauen. Ein Gespräch mit Hermann Czech, Wien," in Tom Schoper, *Ein Haus: Werk – Ding – Zeug?*, 2. ed. (Vienna, 2017), 56 and 58.
8   Ibid, 59.
9   David Ganzoni, "Die Lehre Kollhoffs: Von der Grossform zur Fassade: 25 Jahre lehrte Hans Kollhoff Architektur an der ETH Zürich: Über die Nachwirkungen in der Schweizer Architektur," *Hochparterre* 24, no. 11 (2011), 22–23.

VOM MASTERPLAN ZUR MODULAREN NUTZUNG
Das Departement Bau und Raum KSSG im Interview
Urs Buschor, Marko Sauer, Silvan Schneider, Christof Stäheli

FROM MASTER PLAN TO MODULAR USE
The Department of Building and Planning of KSSG in Interview
Urs Buschor, Marko Sauer, Silvan Schneider, Christof Stäheli

Haus 10, 5. Obergeschoss, Anmelde- und Wartebereich Onkologie/Hämatologie/
Building 10, 5th floor, registration and waiting area oncology/hematology
Fotos/Photo: Florian Brunner

Urs Buschor, Mitglied der Geschäftsleitung KSSG, Leiter Departement Bau und Raum, Vizepräsident im Verwaltungsrat der Spitalanlagengesellschaft.
Urs Buschor, Member of the Executive Board of KSSG, Director of the Department of Building and Planning, Vice Chair of the Construction Project Management Division.

Silvan Schneider, Leiter des Bereichs Bauprojektmanagement KSSG und Projektleiter Bauherr für das Haus 10.
Silvan Schneider, Head of the Construction Project Management Division of KSSG and Project Manager for Building 10.

Christof Stäheli, Architekt mit eigenem Büro in St.Gallen, von 2004 bis 2017 Bauherrenberater KSSG und von 2013 bis 2019 Mitglied und Vorsitzender der Kunstkommission H-Kunst.
Christof Stäheli, architect with his own office in St.Gallen, from 2004 to 2017 Building Consultant for KSSG and from 2013 to 2019 Member and Chairman of the Art Commission H-Kunst.

Marko Sauer (MSa): The renovation of the Cantonal Hospital St.Gallen (KSSG) is a generational project. After a decade of planning, the construction work has now reached its largest stage with the buildings 07A and OKS. How do you set about working on such a huge undertaking?

Christof Stäheli (CSt): We began with an overall feasibility study for the construction. In the 1990s at management retreats we fit in half and whole days to discuss the future building project together with representatives of the KSSG and the head of hospital construction from the cantonal building authority. We also invited several eminent authorities in hospital construction, such as Monika Merki Frey and Heinz Locher. We discussed from the ground up, the direction in which the hospital building could develop and what possibilities that would yield.

Urs Buschor (UBu): There were two levels to this strategy. On the one hand, the mentioned overall feasibility study, which was the precursor to the master plan. There we laid out the basic parameters for the competition, with the construction sites and the buildings that should be maintained. On the other hand, management also discussed the options at an operational level: how will hospitals be positioned in the future? What are the megatrends in healthcare? At the time, the keywords were *population growth*, *aging population*, and *patient hotel*. Over time, *centralization of hospitals* was added to that and soon the keyword *patient-centered*.

MSa: How much of the original master plan is still present in the project?

CSt: The planning was, of course, constantly adapted and customized at each level. Metron Architekten formulated a very flexible master plan, and correctly so. It could have provided the base for several different projects.

UBu: Currently, we're in the master plan's overview of buildings. With regard to the first buildings, however, the plan has remained relatively stable. Only minimal adaptations occurred with regard to the urban planning form and special use plan. The master plan helps us avoid conflicts in the next steps of the long-term overall renovation. Thanks to the plan, we know which construction fields we have to keep open so we don't block later stages of construction.

Silvan Schneider (SSch): And when the master plan is also further implemented, then we already keep fields free for the next generation. This plan shapes a common thread guiding through the KSSG's structural development. Even when

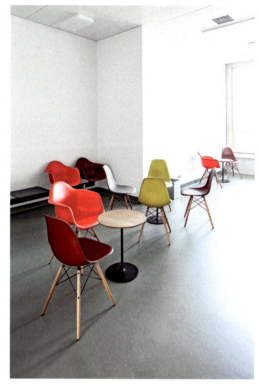

Silvan Schneider (SSch): Wenn der Masterplan auch weiterhin umgesetzt wird, dann halten wir bereits jetzt Felder für die nächste Generation frei. Dieser Plan bildet den roten Faden in der baulichen Entwicklung des KSSG. Auch wenn wir dereinst nicht mehr am Ruder sein werden – die nächste Generation kann diesen Weg weiter beschreiten. Die Entwicklung verläuft im Areal immer gegen den Uhrzeigersinn. Und wenn diese Entwicklung am Ende angekommen ist, kann man wieder von vorne beginnen.

CSt: Dabei ist es wichtig, die betroffenen Felder auch tatsächlich zu räumen und freizuhalten. Zum Beispiel mussten wir nach dem Auszug der alten Pathologie dafür kämpfen, dass das Haus nicht neu belegt wird. Es hätte noch geraume Zeit stehen bleiben können, und es herrscht überall permanenter Platzmangel. Aber man hat auf strategischer Ebene begriffen, dass man diesem Drängen nicht nachgeben darf, weil man sich damit sonst ins eigene Fleisch geschnitten hätte. Wir mussten ein Abbruchgesuch stellen und das Haus rückbauen – acht Jahre, bevor dort Neubauten errichtet werden.

SSch: Es gilt auch heute noch die Prämisse, Häuser möglichst schnell ausser Betrieb zu nehmen und zurückzubauen.

UBu: Dabei gibt es auch noch einen betrieblichen Aspekt. Wenn wir ein Gebäude stehen lassen und dieses mit einer anderen Nutzung belegen, dann müssen wir nach dem Rückbau auch dafür wieder Ersatzflächen anbieten. Und irgendwann schaffen wir es nicht mehr, das nächste Baufeld freizuspielen. Dann wären wir blockiert.

MSa: Der Masterplan bildet also den Basso continuo der Planung und ordnet die Volumetrie der einzelnen Gebäude und wie diese zueinander stehen. Wie kommt man aber von der betrieblichen Vision zu einer räumlichen Vorstellung?

UBu: Wir haben angefangen, umfangreiche Beziehungsmatrizes zu erstellen, die zeigen, wie sich die Zusammenarbeit über das ganze Spital hinweg gestaltet und wie eng dieser Austausch ist. Aus dem Dokument ging die Interaktion der einzelnen Kliniken hervor. Dieses Abbild unserer Organisationsstruktur haben wir abgegeben und den Architekten den Auftrag erteilt, die einzelnen Einheiten in eine sinnvolle Beziehung zueinander zu stellen. Das war neben dem Masterplan ein wichtiges Dokument für den Wettbewerb.

MSa: Wie hat sich diese Matrix auf die Wettbewerbsbeiträge ausgewirkt?

we are no longer at the helm one day, the next generation can continue to follow this path. Development on the site always runs counterclockwise. And when this development has reached its end, it's possible to start from the beginning again.

CSt: At the same time, it's important to truly clear the fields in question and keep them free. For example, after moving out of the old pathology building, we had to put up a fight to stop the building from being reoccupied. It could have remained standing for some time, and there is a shortage of space everywhere. But at a strategic level, we grasped that we shouldn't give in to this pressure, because that would only harm us in the end. We had to apply for a demolition permit and tear down the building—eight years before new buildings were put up there.

SSch: The premise still holds today: pull buildings out of operation as quickly as possible and remove them.

UBu: There's also an operational aspect to this. If we were to leave a building standing and fill it with other uses, then after it's removed we'd also have to provide replacement areas for these uses. And at some point, we'd no longer be able to free up the next construction field. Then we'd be blocked.

MSa: The master plan is thereby the basso continuo of the planning and sorts the volumetric arrangement of the individual buildings and how they position themselves to one another. But how do you move from an operational vision to a spatial conception?

UBu: We started to make extensive matrices of relationships that show how cooperation takes shape throughout the entire hospital and how dense this exchange is. Emerging from this document were the interactions of the individual clinics. We submitted this depiction of our organizational structure to the architects and gave them the job of placing the individual units in a sensible relationship to one another. That was an important document for the competition, along with the master plan.

MSa: How did these matrices affect the competition submissions?

UBu: Also submitted in the first phase was a spatial program in which every clinic was described again as a unit—with offices, spaces for the head physicians, operating rooms, and outpatient clinics. This perspective naturally conflicts with the matrix. The spatial plans of the clinics lasted beyond the judging of the competition, through to the first pre-project.

Baustelle Haus 10, 21.03.2017 / Construction site, Building 10, March 21, 2017
Foto / Photo: Florian Brunner

UBu: In der ersten Phase wurde zusätzlich noch ein Raumprogramm abgegeben, in dem jede Klinik wieder als Einheit beschrieben war – mit Sekretariat, Räumen für die Chefärzte, Operationssälen und Ambulatorium. Diese Sichtweise steht natürlich in einem Spannungsfeld zur Matrix. Der Raumplan der Kliniken hat über die Jurierung des Wettbewerbs hinaus bis ins erste Vorprojekt getragen.

MSa: Was ist danach passiert?

UBu: Im Januar 2017 wurden die Immobilien und das Grundstück vom Kanton an das Kantonsspital übertragen. Damit wechselte unsere Rolle im Projekt vom Nutzer zum Eigentümer und vom Besteller zum Bauherrn. Nun hatten wir die Möglichkeit, alles nochmals zu prüfen und zu überarbeiten. Im Siegerprojekt standen die Kliniken schon sehr vernünftig zueinander. Dank unserer neuen Möglichkeiten als Eigentümer konnten wir jedoch die Organisation, die Prozesse und die Wegeführung innerhalb des Siegerprojekts nochmals genauer untersuchen. Dies geschah im Rahmen der sogenannten Strukturbereinigung.

MSa: Welche Aspekte wurden bei dieser Bereinigung untersucht?

UBu: Das ging ziemlich tief ins Projekt: die Erschliessungsachsen, die Trennung zwischen Patienten- und Logistikwegen bis hin zu den administrativen Flächen, die wir neu als

MSa: What happened afterward?

UBu: In January 2017 the real estate and the property were transferred from the canton to the cantonal hospital. With that, our role in the project changed from user to owner and from customer to client. We now had the chance to look over and rework everything again. In the winning project, the clinics were already placed in a very sensible relationship to one another. But thanks to our new possibilities as owner, we could again take a closer look at the organization, the processes, and route guidance within the winning project. This happened in the context of the so-called structural reassessment.

MSa: What aspects were examined in this reassessment?

UBu: It went quite deep into the project: the access axes, separation of patient and logistic routes, through to the administrative areas, which we now understand as impersonal, open-space areas. But the most fundamental question was: does it all work together?

MSa: You mentioned before the concept of the patient-centered hospital. How should we imagine that?

UBu: The hospital's range of functions are viewed from the perspective of the patient, not from the perspective of the clinics. Basically, in contrast to clinic-centering, with

Haus 10, 4. Obergeschoss, Behandlungsbereich Onkologie/Hämatologie/Building 10, 4th floor, treatment area—oncology/hematology
Fotos/Photos: Florian Brunner

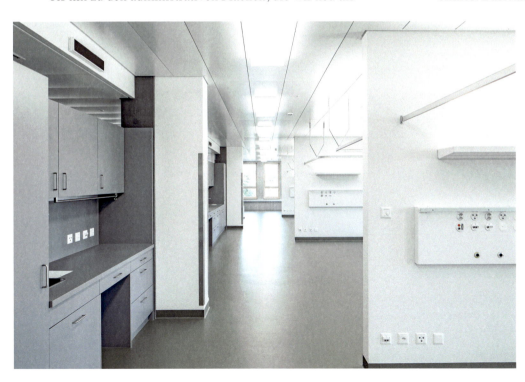
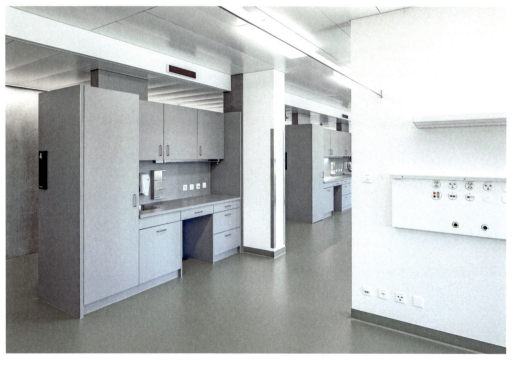

unpersönliche Open-Space-Flächen verstanden. Die grundlegende Frage aber war: Funktioniert das alles zusammen?

MSa: Sie nannten vorhin den Begriff des patientenzentrierten Spitals. Was muss man sich darunter vorstellen?

UBu: Die Funktionalität des Spitals wird aus Sicht des Patienten betrachtet und nicht aus Sicht der Kliniken. Grundsätzlich bei der Patientenzentrierung ist – im Gegensatz zur Klinikzentrierung –, dass man funktional Zusammengehörendes infrastrukturell zueinanderführt.

MSa: Das heisst konkret?

UBu: Der Arzt geht zum Patienten und nicht umgekehrt. Wir denken nicht mehr in Kliniken, sondern gruppieren die Funktionen über das ganze Spitalareal hinweg.

MSa: Und wie äussert sich das?

UBu: Nehmen wir als Beispiel die Kardiologie. Die ist heute im Haus 01 untergebracht. Im Erdgeschoss hat der Chefarzt auf der einen Seite sein Herzkatheterlabor und das Chefarztbüro, auf der anderen Seite sein Ambulatorium für die nicht-invasiven Untersuchungen wie EKG und Schrittmacher, darüber liegt seine Bettenstation. Das ist eine komplette Klinik, die kompakt an einem Ort untergebracht ist. Im neuen Spital ist die Kardiologie aufgeteilt. Dort wird der Kardiologe im ersten Obergeschoss seine Herzkatheter-

patient-centering, what belongs together in terms of function is brought together in the infrastructure.

MSa: And what does that mean concretely?

UBu: The doctor goes to the patient and not vice versa. We no longer think in terms of clinics, but instead group the functions across the entire hospital grounds.

MSa: And how is that expressed?

UBu: Take cardiology, for example. Right now, it is housed in Building 01. On the ground floor, the head physician has on one side his cardiac catheter lab and head physician office; on the other side, his outpatient clinic for noninvasive exams, such as ECG and pacemaker, and the inpatient ward is on the floor above. That is a complete clinic, which is housed compactly on a site. In the new hospital, cardiology is spread out. There, the cardiologist will have his cardiac catheter lab on the first floor; right next to it is the intensive care station. In contrast, he'll have his noninvasive outpatient clinic in the existing Building 03; the inpatient ward in the tower, in Building 07A; and his office will once again be on another site on the grounds.

MSa: That means that the functional connections will no longer be viewed from the perspective of the clinic.

Haus 10, 4. Obergeschoss, Behandlungsbereich Onkologie / Hämatologie / Building 10, 4th floor, treatment area—oncology/hematology
Fotos / Photos: Florian Brunner

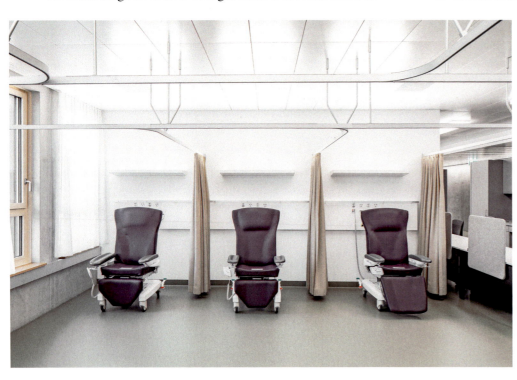
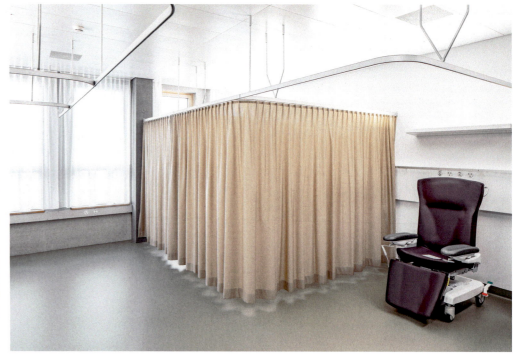

labors haben, gleich daneben kommt die medizinische Intensivstation zu liegen. Sein nicht-invasives Ambulatorium hingegen wird er im bestehenden Haus 03 haben, die Bettenstation liegt im Turm, im Haus 07A, und seine Büros befinden sich nochmals an einem anderen Ort auf dem Areal.

MSa: Das heisst, die funktionalen Zusammenhänge werden nicht mehr aus Sicht der Klinik betrachtet.

UBu: Genau. Der Chefarzt geht aus seinem Cluster heraus und definiert die Rahmenbedingungen: Ich brauche das Herzkatheterlabor neben der Intensivstation; ich brauche mein hochfrequentes Ambulatorium in einem Gebäude mit einer Tagesstation; und meine Bettenstation sollte möglichst nahe an der Intensivstation sein, muss aber nicht zwingend im selben Gebäude liegen. Für den Verlauf einer Krankheit oder eines Notfalls, zum Beispiel bei einem akuten Herzinfarkt, ist es wichtig, dass das Herzkatheterlabor von der zentralen Notfallaufnahme aus schnell erreicht werden kann und dass nach dem Eingriff die Wege zur Intensivstation kurz sind. Bei den Ambulatorien und Bettenstationen dagegen ist es viel wichtiger, dass diese über öffentliche Haupteingangszonen und grosse Liftgruppen einfach erreichbar sind.

CSt: Dahinter steht natürlich ein Kulturwandel im Spital. Das ist ein entscheidender Punkt, und dieser Wandel muss auch von der Geschäftsleitung mitgetragen werden. Erst dann ist es möglich, Konzepte umzusetzen, die sich vom früheren Vorgehen unterscheiden, wo jeder Chefarzt seine Klinik hatte. So wurde zum Beispiel noch 1980 das Hochhaus 04 für vier Kliniken erstellt. Es hatte vier Eingänge und einen Chefarzt-Lift, der vom Erdgeschoss bis ganz nach oben fuhr und ausschliesslich für die vier Klinikleiter zur Verfügung stand. Das war funktional höchst fragwürdig.

UBu: Und in diesem Turm gab es zudem für die beiden operativen Kliniken zwei Operationssäle, die nicht auf demselben Stock lagen und auch nicht direkt übereinander. Zudem waren dort vier Bettenstationen untergebracht, die nicht das gleiche Layout hatten – für vier Kliniken im selben Gebäude.

MSa: Und wer bestimmt heute, wie das Spital organisiert ist?

UBu: Auf der Ebene der Gesamtprojektleitung haben wir mit den Nutzervertretern nochmals den Blick auf die Struktur der Gebäude gerichtet und darauf, wie die Gebäude untereinander verbunden sind. Die Achsen mussten stimmen, horizontal wie vertikal, mit den Steigschächten, der Versorgung

UBu: Exactly. The head physician leaves his cluster and defines the framework conditions: I need the cardiac catheter lab next to the intensive care station; I need my heavily frequented outpatient clinic in a building with an outpatient ward; and my inpatient ward should be as close to the intensive care station as possible, but does not have to necessarily be in the same building. For the course of an illness or an emergency, for example, in the case of an acute heart attack, it is important that the cardiac catheter lab can be reached quickly from the central emergency room, and that after the operation, the intensive care station is close by. For the outpatient clinics and inpatient wards, on the contrary, it is much more important that they are easily reached via public main entry zones and large groups of lifts.

CSt: Of course, this is motived by a cultural transformation in the hospital. That's a crucial point, and management also has to go along with this transformation. Only then can concepts be realized that differ from previous approaches in which every head physician had his or her clinic. For example, even in 1980 the high-rise Building 04 was built for four clinics. It had four entries and one head physician lift, which went from the ground floor up to the very top and was available exclusively for the four clinic heads. That was highly questionable in terms of function.

UBu: The tower also had two operating rooms for the two operating clinics, but they were not on the same floor and also not directly above one another. Furthermore, four inpatient wards that did not have the same layout were accommodated—for four clinics in the same building.

MSa: And who determines how the hospital is organized nowadays?

UBu: At the level of overall project management, we again looked together with the user representatives at the structure of the buildings and how they are connected with one another. The axes had to conform with the riser shafts, horizontally and vertically, and the supply and logistics throughout all three functional levels. With the users, we then had to fine-tune everything again in the new context. That means the users had to specify and situate their spatial programs three times: first in the competition phase, then in the first pre-project, and a third time on the occasion of the structural reassessment.

Baustelle Haus 10, 21.03.2017 / Construction site, Building 10, March 21, 2017
Foto / Photo: Florian Brunner

und Logistik durch alle drei funktionalen Ebenen hindurch. Mit den Nutzern haben wir im neuen Kontext dann alles nochmals richtig einpassen müssen. Das heisst, die Nutzer mussten ihr Raumprogramm dreimal neu angeben und verorten: zuerst in der Wettbewerbsphase, dann im ersten Vorprojekt und ein drittes Mal anlässlich der Strukturbereinigung.

SSch: Das ist sehr anspruchsvoll für die Nutzer, aber aus meiner Erfahrung ist dies nicht spezifisch für den Spitalbau. Ich würde sagen, das ist oft so bei Grossprojekten, die über mehrere Jahrzehnte hinweg geplant und erstellt werden.

MSa: Wie würden Sie das Spital heute aus Sicht des Patienten beschreiben? Was hat sich durch diesen Wechsel des Blickwinkels verändert und welchen Grundannahmen folgen Sie dabei?

UBu: Es gibt zwei wichtige Prämissen: Erstens haben wir festgehalten, dass es drei funktionale Ebenen gibt – das Erdgeschoss ist die Eintrittspforte ins Spital, hoch frequentiert, eine offene und möglichst freie Zone. Sie ist niedrig installiert und wird ambulant genutzt. Das erste Obergeschoss ist hingegen nur noch halb durchlässig. Dort kann man sich zwar noch selbst bewegen, aber nicht überall. Es ist hochinstalliert, hoch frequentiert, sehr personalintensiv, und es beherbergt die ganzen Interventionsräume, Eingriffe, Untersuchungen sowie Überwachungs- und Behandlungsräume wie Herzkatheterlabors und Endoskopien. Dort liegen aber auch die Tagesstationen, die Intensivstationen, die extrem personalintensiv und technologiegetrieben sind, mit hohem Besucher- und Patientenaufkommen. Die dritte Ebene bildet ein hochinstalliertes, geschlossenes Geschoss. Das ist die Ebene mit den Operationssälen. Diese funktionalen Schichten werden auch im Neubau des Ostschweizer Kinderspitals (OKS) übernommen, soweit dies möglich ist. Das Untergeschoss wiederum ist näher am Eingang, und es bietet eine ruhigere Atmosphäre. Dort befinden sich die Radiologie, die Kapelle und die Hörsäle, zudem Rückzugsmöglichkeiten wie der Ort der Stille. Ab dem zweiten Untergeschoss gibt es dann nur noch Technik- und Logistikflächen.

MSa: Und was ist die zweite Prämisse?

UBu: Wir haben die Kernzone neu definiert. Was am unterirdischen Kanalsystem angeschlossen ist und was patientengängig ist, gehört zur Kernzone. Diese ist primär für die Patienten reserviert. Dort lassen sich Ambulatorien oder

SSch: That's very challenging for the users, but in my experience, it's not specific to hospital construction. I would say that it's often the case for larger projects that are planned and built across several decades.

MSa: How would you describe the hospital today from the point of view of the patient? What has changed through this switch in perspectives and what underlying assumptions go along with that?

UBu: There are two important premises: first, we have ascertained that there are three functional levels—the ground floor is the entry gate into the hospital, highly frequented, an open zone that is as open as possible. It does not have special equipment and is used for outpatients. The first floor, on the contrary, is only semitransparent. You can still walk around on your own there, but not everywhere. It is highly specialized, highly frequented, very staff-intensive, and it houses all of the intervention spaces for operations, examinations, as well as for observation and treatments, such as the cardiac catheter lab and endoscopy. But the outpatient stations are also there, the intensive care stations, which are extremely staff-intensive and technology-driven, with large visitor and patient traffic. The third floor is a highly specialized closed floor. That is the level with the operating rooms. This functional layering has also been adopted as far as possible for the new Children's Hospital of Eastern Switzerland (OKS). The basement level, for its part, is closer to the entry and offers a calmer atmosphere. Located there are radiology, the chapel, lecture halls, as well as possibilities to find some privacy, such as the quiet zone. The second basement level and below are reserved for technology and logistic areas.

MSa: And what is the second premise?

UBu: We have redefined the core zone. Everything that is attached to the underground canal system and is accessible by patients, belongs to the core zone. This is primarily reserved for the patients. Outpatient clinics and inpatient wards can be run there, the administration is shifted to the periphery. And by administration we mean everything that is not tied to permanent contact with patients—for example, the doctors' offices and offices for the nursing management. For them, we have either rented spaces or converted buildings within a five-minute radius of the grounds. Meanwhile, there are clinics in which the entire department—from the head physician to the in-

Baustelle Haus 10, 11.05.2018 / Construction site, Building 10, May 11, 2018

Haus 10, Haupttreppenhaus / Building 10, main stairway
Fotos / Photos: Florian Brunner

Bettenstationen führen, die Administration wird an die Peripherie verlegt. Und unter Administration verstehen wir alles, was nicht mit permanentem Patientenkontakt verbunden ist – also zum Beispiel auch die Ärztebüros und die Pflegeleitungsbüros. Für die haben wir in einem Fünf-Minuten-Radius um das Areal herum entweder Räume zugemietet oder Häuser umgebaut. Mittlerweile gibt es Kliniken, bei denen die ganze Abteilung – vom Chefarzt bis zu den Assistenzärzten – über keine persönlichen Büros mehr in der Kernzone verfügt.

MSa: Also wie im Haus 10, bei dem sich an den Enden jeweils ein Gemeinschaftsbüro befindet.

SSch: Genau. Dort haben wir dies mit den Open-Space-Strukturen beispielhaft umgesetzt. Man teilt sich die Sitzungszimmer und Büroplätze, die ganz bewusst mehrfach belegt werden. Wie bei jeder Neuerung braucht es eine gewisse Zeit, bis sich alles einspielt und die Nutzerinnen und Nutzer den Mehrwert annehmen. Aber die Strategie ist nun im Alltag angekommen, und das Haus 10 ist für uns ein guter Botschafter. Das hilft uns auch beim Neubau der Häuser 07A und 07B.

CSt: Seit sechs Jahren sitzt nun selbst der Direktor des Spitals in diesem Fünf-Minuten-Radius und nicht mehr im repräsentativen Haus 20, weil dieses ebenfalls zur Kernzone gehört. Zuvor hatte dies die Direktion für sich beansprucht.

MSa: Und da hat niemand reklamiert?

UBu: Nein. Der Direktor hat diese Entscheidung mitgetragen. Er meinte, wir leben das, was gilt, und das gelte auch für ihn.

MSa: Die beiden Prämissen – funktionale Ebenen und Kernzone – ordnen die betrieblichen Aspekte des Spitals. Wie schaffen Sie es aber, die ständig wechselnden Bedürfnisse der Medizin innerhalb dieser Struktur aufzufangen?

UBu: Die Grundlage bilden das Gebäuderaster und flexible Anschlussmöglichkeiten in der Fassade. Wir nutzen ein flexibles Industrieraster für die Tragstruktur mit 8.10 Metern Achsmass. Das zweite ist die Setzung der vertikalen Erschliessungskerne.

MSa: Welche Flexibilität bietet die Struktur innerhalb des Rasters?

UBu: Wir haben verschiedene Grundraumtypen definiert: das Untersuchungszimmer, das am häufigsten vorkommt, und die Spezialuntersuchungszimmer, die sich am schnellsten entwickeln. Daneben gibt es Operationssäle, Wartezonen und administrative Flächen. Viel mehr gibt es eigentlich nicht. Innerhalb der Grundstruktur lassen sich die Räume

terns—no longer have personal offices available in the core zone.

MSa: Like in Building 10, where an open-space office is located at each of the ends.

SSch: Exactly. There we implemented it with open-space structures to set an example. The meeting rooms and office spaces are shared and intentionally have multiple functions. As with every innovation, it takes a certain amount of time until everything falls into place and the users accept the added value. But the strategy is now integrated in daily life, and Building 10 is a good ambassador for us. That also helps us in the new construction of Buildings 07A and 07B.

CSt: For six years now, even the director of the hospital has been located in this five-minute radius and is no longer in the representative Building 20, because it is also part of the core zone. Before, the management claimed this building for itself.

MSa: And no one has complained about it?

UBu: No. The director supported this decision. He said that this is the way we're doing things, and that applies to him, too.

MSa: The two premises—functional levels and core zones—organize the operational aspects of the hospital. But how do you manage to absorb medicine's constantly changing demands within this structure?

UBu: The basis is the building grid and flexible connection possibilities in the façade. We use a flexible industrial grid for the support structure with an 8.10-meter axis dimension. Second is the placement of the vertical access cores.

MSa: What flexibility does the structure offer within the grid?

UBu: We defined various types of basic spaces: exam rooms, which are the most common, and the special exam rooms, which develop the fastest. In addition, there are operating rooms, waiting areas, and administrative areas. There actually isn't a lot more. Within the basic structure, the spaces can be put together in various ways. From these elements—and that then goes into corporate development—we developed standard modules for an outpatient clinic with service points, waiting areas, and standard and special examination rooms. We use these modules for the new buildings as well as for the existing buildings.

MSa: These modules are then comparable for every clinic.

UBu: Exactly. They can be linked together and adapted, depending on how a department develops. Two normal examination rooms can be put together to make a special room without

variabel zusammenfügen. Wir haben aus diesen Elementen – und das geht dann in die Unternehmensentwicklung hinein – Standardmodule entwickelt für ein Ambulatorium mit Anlaufpunkten, Wartepunkten, Standard- und Spezialuntersuchungszimmern. Wir verwenden diese Module für die Neubauten ebenso wie für Bauten im Bestand.

MSa: Diese Module sind dann für jede Klinik vergleichbar.

UBu: Genau. Sie lassen sich aneinanderkoppeln und anpassen, je nachdem, wie sich eine Abteilung entwickelt. Denn aus zwei normalen Untersuchungszimmern lässt sich ohne grossen Aufwand ein Spezialzimmer erstellen. Als Konstante kommt in einem gewissen Rhythmus wieder eine Anmelde- oder Wartezone. Es gibt also nicht mehr eine grosse Klinik mit dreissig Untersuchungszimmern und einer Administration und daneben eine kleine Abteilung mit nur drei Zimmern und einer eigenen Administration, sondern die Kliniken nutzen zugeteilte Kontingente dieser Standardmodule. In diesem Grundraster, das dank seiner Tiefe flexibel einsetzbar ist, lässt sich die Entwicklung der Kliniken auffangen. Wenn sich die Bedürfnisse verändern, bedeutet das nicht jedes Mal einen Umbau, sondern man kann einen Raum einfach neu zuordnen.

MSa: Dieses Konzept lässt sich auch im Haus 10 beobachten?

SSch: Baulich wurde dort ein Grossteil dieses Konzepts umgesetzt. Die drei Stichworte sind Leichtbauwände, die sich einfach anpassen lassen, Raumhöhen, dank derer man unter den Hohldecken nachinstallieren kann, und der Verzicht auf Bodenheizungen, damit man beim Bohren nicht die Heizung beschädigt. Nutzungsänderungen lassen sich daher mit verhältnismässig geringem Aufwand umsetzen. Flexible Raster und Bauweisen sind aber auch in der Industrie oder bei Bürobauten bekannt, wo diese ebenfalls gefordert sind.

CSt: Man kann sagen, dass das Haus 10 so etwas wie ein Übungshaus für diese Strategie geworden ist.

MSa: Ist neben der Medizin auch in anderen Bereichen mit Veränderungen zu rechnen, für die man Flexibilität bieten muss?

UBu: Bei den Bettenstationen ist die Veränderung natürlich viel geringer als bei den interventionellen Flächen. Eine Bettenstation bleibt sich in etwa gleich. Da ist eher der Betrieb gefordert: Informatik, Lüftung, Entsorgung, Steigzonen, Wärme und Kälte, Reinigungskonzepte, automatisiertes Versorgungskonzept, Rohrpost, zukünftige Formen der Kommunikation, Patiententerminals, Prozessunter-

any great effort. A registration or waiting zone occurs in a certain rhythm, as a constant. So there's no longer a large clinic with thirty examination rooms and an administration and, next to it, a small department with only three rooms and its own administration, but instead the clinics use their assigned quota of these standard modules. In this basic grid, which owing to its depth can be flexibly deployed, it's possible to keep up with the development of the clinics. So every time needs change, that doesn't mean conversion is necessary; instead, it's possible to simply reallocate a space.

MSa: Can this concept be observed now in Building 10?

SSch: A great deal of this concept has been realized there in terms of structure. The three keywords are: lightweight construction walls, which can be adapted easily; room heights, thanks to which installations can be added later under a false ceiling; and doing without floor heating, so that the heating is not damaged when drilling. Changes in use can thus be implemented with a relatively low effort. Flexible grids and building methods, however, are also common in industrial and office buildings, where they are likewise required.

CSt: One could say that Building 10 has become a type of practice building for this strategy.

MSa: Are changes expected in other areas apart from medicine, for which flexibility has to be offered?

UBu: With inpatient wards, there is naturally much less change than with interventional areas. An inpatient ward remains approximately the same. What's demanding there, instead, are the operational aspects: informatics, ventilation, waste disposal, riser shafts, heating and air conditioning, cleaning concepts, automated care concepts, pneumatic post, future forms of communication, patient terminals, and process support, etc. These are all themes that accompany a building and for which one has to look ten years ahead into the future because a generation is skipped in each case.

SSch: This development—technologically and operationally—is often also promoted by construction. We're always in a charged field, because when building we want to account for new processes and technologies so that the infrastructure is sustainable for the future.

UBu: In these areas, it was often challenging to make a statement. In ten years, there'll still be operations in the medical field. But at the level of building technology, no one can say where we'll be in a decade. We don't know what

Baustelle Haus 10, 11.05.2018 / Construction site, Building 10, May 11, 2018
Foto / Photo: Florian Brunner

stützung etc. Das sind alles Themen, die mit einem Bau einhergehen und bei denen man ebenfalls auf zehn Jahre hinaus in die Zukunft schauen muss, weil es da jeweils einen Generationensprung gibt.

SSch: Oft wird diese Entwicklung – technologisch und betrieblich – auch durch den Bau vorangetrieben. Da steht man immer in einem Spannungsfeld, weil wir beim Bauen neue Prozesse und Technologien berücksichtigen wollen, damit die Infrastruktur zukunftsfähig bleibt.

UBu: In diesen Bereichen war es häufig anspruchsvoll, eine Aussage zu machen. In der Medizin wird man auch in zehn Jahren noch operieren. Aber auf der Ebene der Haustechnik konnte uns niemand sagen, wo wir in einem Jahrzehnt stehen werden. Wir wissen nicht, was 2030 der Standard sein wird bezüglich Telefonie, Kommunikation oder Raumsteuerung. Aber wir mussten zum Beispiel entscheiden, ob wir für die Medien konventionell mit Kabeln einfahren oder gleich auf LAN oder WLAN setzen. Das sind Grundprinzipien, die bei Baubeginn festgelegt werden müssen.

SSch: Auch da haben wir reagiert, indem wir in den Steigzonen eine gewisse Reserve eingeplant haben. Dies ermöglicht Nachinstallationen, um auf geänderte Bedürfnisse und Anforderungen reagieren zu können. Solche Vorleistungen

the standard will be in 2030 in terms of telephone services, communication, or room control. But we had to decide, for example, whether to go in conventionally with cables for media, or rely directly on LAN and WLAN. These are basic principles that have to be established at the start of construction.

SSch: We also reacted there in that we planned a certain reserve in the riser shafts. This allows for later installations in order to react to changed needs and demands. Such preliminary work pays off in the future—it enables easy reinstallation to keep up with technological developments.

MSa: A hospital can be realized as a building development or on a greenfield. Would it have been an advantage for the planning if you could have started at zero?

UBu: Building redevelopment is, of course, much more complex. That's evident in all aspects that we've discussed. At the same time, the potential is also much greater because we have to constantly react at every stage. If we would have had to define and decide all at once what the medical field would look like in thirty years, we would have spent a billion Swiss francs in the shortest time possible and created nine hundred beds in all of the outpatient clinics. There's a lot of risk in determining operational demands all at

Haus 10, Liftvorbereiche / Building 10, area in front of lifts
Fotos / Photos: Georg Aerni

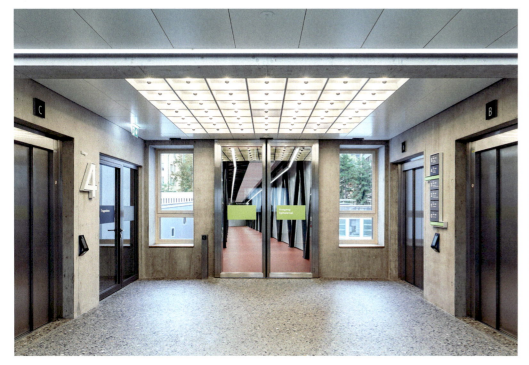

zahlen sich in Zukunft aus, sie ermöglichen die einfache Nachinstallation aufgrund technologischer Entwicklungen.

MSa: Ein Spital kann man im Bestand realisieren oder auf der grünen Wiese. Wäre es für Ihre Planungen ein Vorteil gewesen, wenn Sie bei null hätten anfangen können?

UBu: Das Bauen im Bestand ist natürlich viel aufwendiger. Das sieht man an allen Aspekten, die wir besprochen haben. Zugleich ist aber auch das Potenzial viel grösser, weil wir bei jeder Etappe wieder reagieren können. Wenn wir auf einen Schlag definieren und entscheiden müssten, wie die Medizin in dreissig Jahren aussieht, würden wir in kürzester Zeit eine Milliarde Franken verbauen und neunhundert Betten mit allen Ambulatorien erstellen. Es liegt ein grosses Risiko darin, die betrieblichen Anforderungen auf einen Schlag festzulegen. Zum Beispiel haben wir entschieden, dass es nur noch Einzelzimmer gibt, und darauf konnten wir dann mit dem Raster reagieren.

SSch: Die grüne Wiese mag für ein kleineres Spital funktionieren. Aber bei einem Zentrumsspital trifft man auf völlig andere Dimensionen.

CSt: Es gibt in Europa mehrere Projekte, die aufgrund ihrer Grösse und Komplexität einfach nicht fertig werden. Das hat mit vielem zu tun, aber die Komplexität hat zur once. For example, we decided that there will be only single rooms, and we can react to that with the grid.

SSch: The greenfield might work for a smaller hospital. But with a regional hospital, you encounter entirely different dimensions.

CSt: There are several projects in Europe that will simply never be finished due to their size and complexity. That has to do with a lot of things, but because of the complexity, a single error in planning can have enormous consequences. Building redevelopment corresponds more with our mentality because it limits urban growth. You put a stop to something, replace it, build new. In St.Gallen we are fortunate to have a very generous solution with a new building that connects the entire grounds.

UBu: Building on a greenfield also entails newly creating all of the labs, institutes, bus stations, connections with streets, etc. You would have to maintain and further operate all existing structures until moving day, following all regulations, as it would not be possible to slowly phase out business. And then, finally, there aren't any customers for hospital real estate. That means, you have to swallow seven hundred million to a billion Swiss francs and write it all off at once. There's no way to finance that.

Haus 10, Netzersatzanlage / Building 10, emergency power system
Fotos / Photos: Florian Brunner

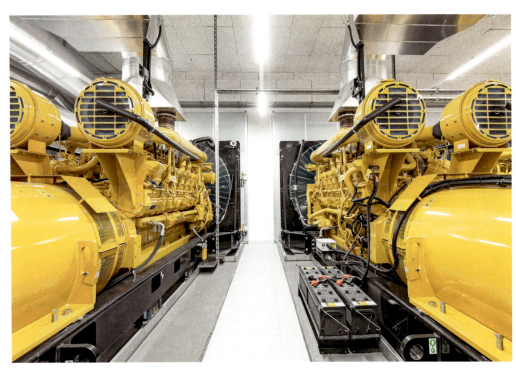

Folge, dass ein einziger Planungsfehler enorme Auswirkungen haben kann. Das Bauen im Bestand entspricht auch mehr unserer Mentalität, weil es ein städtebauliches Wachstum bedingt. Man bricht etwas ab, ersetzt, baut neu. Wir haben in St.Gallen das Glück, dass wir eine sehr grosszügige Lösung haben mit einem Neubau, der das ganze Areal verbindet.

UBu: Mit einem Bau auf der grünen Wiese geht zudem einher, dass alle Labors, Institute, Busstationen, Anschlüsse an Strassen etc. neu erstellt werden müssen. Man müsste sämtliche bestehenden Strukturen bis zum Tag des Umzugs unter Einhaltung aller Vorschriften aufrechterhalten und weiterbetreiben, denn es wäre nicht möglich, den Betrieb langsam herunterzufahren. Und am Ende gibt es dann keinen Käufer für die Spitalimmobilien. Das heisst, man müsste siebenhundert Millionen bis zu einer Milliarde Franken vernichten, und alles auf einen Schlag abschreiben. Das ist nicht finanzierbar.

MSa: Was kann man betrieblich vom Projekt in St.Gallen lernen? Ist es der Kulturwandel? Oder ist das schon Common Sense?

UBu: Von aussen kommt oft die Rückmeldung, dass wir kulturell fortschrittlich sind und dass die interdisziplinäre Zusammenarbeit im Vergleich zu anderen grossen Spitälern weit gediehen ist. Das Bauen treibt diese Entwicklung voran, weil Fragen zur angestrebten Zusammenarbeit beantwortet werden müssen, bevor man das Layout der Neubauten festlegt. Genau diese Fragestellungen wurden mit dem Bauprojekt und der Überprüfung der Bestellung nochmals akzentuiert untersucht. In dieser Phase hat die Unternehmensentwicklung die Verantwortung für die Erstellung der zukünftigen Betriebskonzepte übernommen.

CSt: In den letzten Jahren gab es zudem auch einige innovative Köpfe, die sich gegenseitig befruchtet haben, wie zum Beispiel in der Radiologie. In den Regionalspitälern entstehen die Bilder, in St.Gallen werden dann zentral die Befunde erstellt. Das sind Formen der Zusammenarbeit, die man sich vor zehn Jahren noch nicht hätte vorstellen können. Der Wandel wird am Kantonsspital St.Gallen immer gefördert und man begrüsst ihn. Es gibt hier offenbar nur wenige Bremser.

MSa: What can we learn operationally from the project in St.Gallen? Is it a cultural transformation? Or is that actually common sense?

UBu: We often get the feedback from outside that we're progressive in terms of culture, and that the interdisciplinary cooperation is much more extensive in comparison with other large hospitals. The building propels this development because questions about the desired cooperation have to be answered before establishing the layout of the new buildings. Precisely these issues are highlighted once again with the building project and the verification of the commission. In this phase, corporate development has assumed responsibility for generating future operational concepts.

CSt: Recently, there have also been several innovative minds that have mutually enriched one another, for example, in radiology. Images are made in regional hospitals, then reports are created centrally in St.Gallen. Ten years ago, it wasn't even possible to imagine these forms of cooperation. At the Cantonal Hospital St.Gallen, change will always be supported and also welcomed. Apparently, there aren't many holding things back here.

Baustelle Haus 10, 11.05.2018 / Construction site, Building 10, May 11, 2018
Foto / Photo: Florian Brunner

DER KONTEXT BESTIMMT DEN ENTWURF
Clementine Hegner-van Rooden

CONTEXT DETERMINES DESIGN
Clementine Hegner-van Rooden

Ausführungspläne Passerelle, Schneider Stahlbau AG / Implementation plans of aerial walkway, Schneider Stahlbau AG

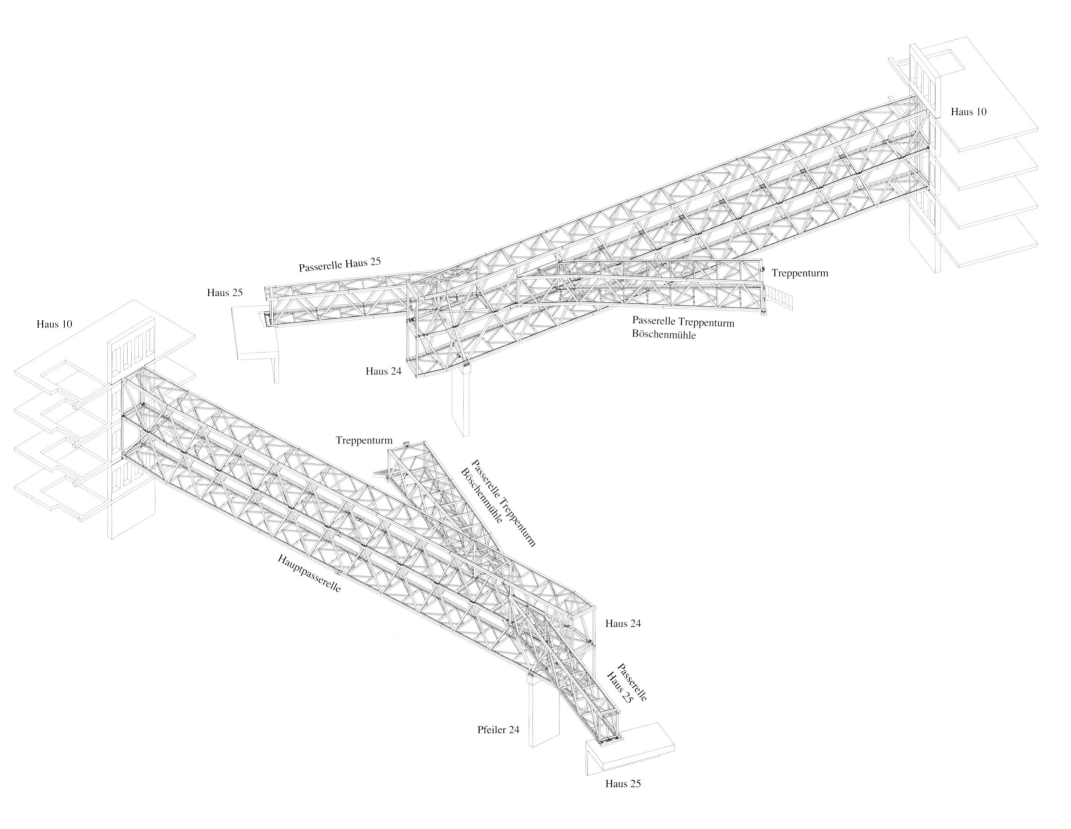

Der Entwurf einer Brücke erfordert eine hohe Sensibilität für unterschiedliche, teils widersprüchliche Rahmenbedingungen, egal ob die Brücke in einer sensiblen Landschaft oder im innerstädtischen Bereich steht. Jede einzelne Rahmenbedingung beeinflusst den Entwurfsprozess, mit jeder Bedingung, die berücksichtigt wird, entwickeln sich das Tragwerk und die Architektur weiter, jede zu befolgende Angabe verändert das Modell, jeder Kontext prägt und gestaltet die Konstruktion. Letztlich ist es die Verknüpfung aller Erfordernisse, die einer Brücke ihren ganz eigenen Charakter gibt. Die Passerelle auf dem Areal des Kantonsspitals St.Gallen veranschaulicht plastisch, wie analysierte funktionale Anforderungen sowie einzuhaltende architektonische und ingenieurspezifische Bedingungen den Entwurf substanziell bestimmen.

MASSGESCHNEIDERT EINGEBETTET

Die neue Passerelle hat die geometrische Form eines liegenden X, das gekonnt den Neubau des Hauses 10 bzw. den Treppenturm des Parkhauses Böschenmühle mit dem bestehenden Spitalareal verknüpft. Die umständlichen Wege über den Wind und Wetter ausgesetzten öffentlichen Bereich mit der zu überquerenden Lindenstrasse entfallen, und es entstehen direkte, ebenerdige Verbindungswege für den Besucher- und den Patientenverkehr.

Die geometrische Form ist unregelmässig mit unterschiedlich langen Schenkeln, variablen Breiten und Höhen. Einer der Schenkel ist zweigeschossig ausgebildet, der andere über die ganze Länge eingeschossig. Während die obere Ebene der Brücke öffentlich ist und dem Personenverkehr gehört, ist die untere Ebene dem Bettentransport vorbehalten. Sie führt als gerade Linie vom vierten Obergeschoss des Hauses 10 zum Haus 24a. Der öffentliche Bereich wird mit dieser vertikalen Schichtung strikt von den Patienten- und Logistikbereichen getrennt, was Raum für reibungslose Abläufe und einen abgesicherten Patientenbereich ohne Publikumsverkehr schafft.

Das 46 Meter weit spannende Haupttragwerk bildet den zweigeschossigen Balken mit einer Gesamtlänge von über 50 Metern. Es ist in Form eines Einfeldträgers mit einer einseitigen Auskragung von rund 5 Metern ausgebildet. Der Träger weist im Achsmass des Tragwerks eine Gesamthöhe von 7.82 Metern und eine Breite von 2.95 Metern auf. Der eingeschossige einheitlich 3.46 Meter hohe Abzweiger zum Treppenturm ist rund 19 Meter lang, jener zum Haus 25 etwa 16 Meter. Die Breite der Träger variiert zwischen schmalen 1.84 Metern bei Haus 25 und grosszügigen 3.00 Metern bei Haus 10 bzw. 3.53 Metern beim Treppenturm. Die Abmessungen spiegeln das einengende Einfädeln

Regardless of whether a bridge is located in a sensitive landscape or within a city, its design must be highly sensible to diverse, in part contradictory, basic conditions. Every framework condition influences the design process: with every condition that is factored in, the support structure and architecture are further developed; every specification changes the model; and every context influences and shapes the construction. In the end, the linking of all demands is what gives a bridge its own personal character. The aerial walkway on the grounds of the Cantonal Hospital St.Gallen vividly demonstrates how greatly the design is determined by analyzed functional demands and architecture and engineering-specific conditions.

CUSTOM EMBEDDED

The new aerial walkway has the geometric form of a horizontal X, which skillfully links the new structure of Building 10—that is, the Böschenmühle parking garage's stair tower—with the existing hospital grounds. Direct, ground-level connecting routes for visitor and patient traffic are created, replacing the inconvenient, wind- and weather-exposed route over the public area, and the crossing of Lindenstrasse.

The geometric shape is irregular with different-sized flanks and variable widths and heights. One of the flanks is developed as two-story, the other is one-story throughout its entire length. While the upper level of the bridge is public and designated for foot traffic, the lower level is reserved for bed transport. It leads as a direct line from the fourth floor of Building 10 to Building 24a. With this vertical layering, the public area is strictly separated from the patient and logistics area, creating space for smooth flows and a secured patient area with no public traffic.

The main supporting structure, spanning 46 meters, is formed by the two-story girders with a total length of more than 50 meters. It is developed in the shape of a single-span girder with a one-sided cantilever of roughly 5 meters. In the axis dimensions of the supporting structure, the carrier features a total height of 7.82 meters and a width of 2.95 meters. The single-story, uniformly 3.46-meter-high branch to the stair tower is around 19 meters long; the branch to Building 25, about 16 meters. The width of the carrier varies between a narrow 1.84 meters for Building 25 and a generous 3 meters for Building 10, and 3.53 meters for the stair tower. The dimensions reflect, on the one hand, the narrowing threading in between the existing buildings, and on the other hand, the realizable generous gesture of the new construction. The two single-story flanks function statically as simple girders.

Baustelle Passerelle, 17.07.2017 / Construction site, aerial walkway, July 17, 2017
Fotos / Photos: Florian Brunner

zwischen den Bestandsbauten auf der einen sowie die umsetzbare grosszügige Geste beim Neubau auf der anderen Seite wider. Die beiden eingeschossigen Schenkel funktionieren statisch als einfache Balken.

Gelagert sind sie einerseits auf dem Haupttragwerk, andererseits auf den Auflagern beim Treppenturm bzw. dem Haus 25. Die Kreuzungsstelle liegt auf einer Betonstützenscheibe von 3 Metern Breite, 8 Metern Höhe und 0.50 Metern Stärke und ist fundiert auf Mikropfählen. Sie ist unmittelbar vor dem Zugang zum Haus 24a bzw. beim Haus 25 angeordnet, ausreichend von der Lindenstrasse zurückversetzt und trägt Vertikal- und Horizontallasten in Querrichtung ab. Gleiches gilt beim Treppenturm Parking Böschenmühle und beim Haus 25. Die Konstruktion ist zudem auf der Seite des Neubaus allseitig fest gelagert, womit sowohl horizontale als auch vertikale Kräfte abgetragen werden können. Auf der Seite des bestehenden Gebäudes Haus 24a ist der auskragende Schenkel allseits verschieblich angeschlossen, denn wegen der schwer abschätzbaren Tragreserven wollte man hier keine zusätzlichen Kräfte abgeben. Infolge Temperaturänderungen entsteht eine relative Verschiebung zwischen Brücke und Bestandsbau von ± 25 Millimetern, im Erdbebenfall können es bis zu ± 40 Millimeter sein. Die Ingenieure haben am Übergang daher eine Fuge vorgesehen, die diese Bewegungen zulässt.

Die Koordination für die effektive Positionierung der Brücke mit ihren Anknüpfstellen war nicht selbsterklärend. Es galt, in einem sich zeitlich verändernden Bau- und damit auch Betriebsprozess die optimale statische, verkehrsspezifische und logistische Lösung zu finden. So war nicht von Beginn an klar, dass der Neubau für eine Lebensdauer von über zehn Jahren ausgelegt würde. Zuerst war er vielmehr als provisorisches Rochadegebäude geplant, das – ebenso wie die Passerelle – eine wesentlich geringere Lebensdauer zu erfüllen gehabt hätte als die fünfzig Jahre Nutzungsdauer konventioneller Hochbauten. Dieses Upgrade und die entsprechende langfristigere Nutzung bedingten andere Verkehrsführungen und Passerellenanschlüsse.

TRAGKONSTRUKTION IN SICH SCHLÜSSIG UND BEGRÜNDET

Das statische System bedingte zusammen mit der relativ grossen Spannweite eine gewichtsreduzierte Konstruktion. Das Planungsteam materialisierte die Passerelle deshalb von Anfang an als leichten Stahlbau, der insgesamt nur 125 Tonnen wiegt. Jeder Schenkel besteht aus einem geschlossenen Stahlfachwerkkasten mit Diagonalen in Boden, Decke, Dach und Seitenwänden.

On one side they are mounted on the main supporting structure; on the other side, on the supports of the stair tower and Building 25. Their intersection is on a concrete support ring that is 3 meters wide, 8 meters high, 0.5 meters thick, and grounded on pin piles. The support ring, which is assigned to Building 25, is located in front of the entrance to Building 24a; is adequately recessed from Lindenstrasse; and dissipates vertical and horizontal loads in a cross direction. The same applies to the Böschenmühle parking garage stair tower and Building 25. The construction is also permanently mounted on the side of the new building, whereby both horizontal as well as vertical forces can be dissipated. On the side of the existing 24a building, the projecting flank is connected flexibly on all sides, as, due to the difficulty of estimating the reserve load capacity, the idea was not to surrender any additional forces. As a result of temperature changes, a relative shift of ± 25 millimeters arises between the bridge and the existing building; in the case of an earthquake, it could be as many as ± 40 millimeters. Therefore, for the transition, the engineers planned a joint that allows for these movements.

The coordination for the effective positioning of the bridge with its connecting points was not self-explanatory. The optimal static, traffic-specific, and logistical solutions had to be found for a time-variable construction and therefore also operational process. From the start, it was not clear that the new building was to be designed for a life-span of more than ten years. The initial plan was for a highly flexible provisional building, which—along with the aerial walkway—would have had to achieve a substantially shorter life-span than the fifty years of use of conventional high-rises. This upgrade and the corresponding long-term use determined different traffic patterns and aerial walkway connections.

SUPPORTING CONSTRUCTION, COHESIVE AND WELL-FOUNDED

The static system, together with the relatively large span width, determined a low-weight construction. The planning team therefore materialized the aerial walkway from the start as a lightweight steel structure, which weighs a total of only 125 tons. Every flank comprises a closed steel truss construction with diagonals in the floor, ceiling, roof, and side walls. The load-bearing elements comprise square pipes (steel grade S355J2G3). The belts are, as a rule, 20 × 20 centimeters large, the diagonals 15 × 15 centimeters. The cross-section sizes, adjusted to one another, enable an aesthetically cohesive profile assemblage. At the same time, in

Haus 10, Passerelle / Building 10, aerial walkway
Fotos / Photos: Florian Brunner

Die Tragelemente bestehen aus Vierkantrohren (Stahlqualität S355J2G3). Die Gurte sind in der Regel 20 × 20 Zentimeter gross, die Diagonalen 15 × 15 Zentimeter. Die aufeinander abgestimmten Querschnittsgrössen ermöglichen ein gestalterisch schlüssiges Zusammenfügen der Profile. Dabei sind die Fachwerke in der Ansicht der Kastenträger als reine Strebenfachwerke ohne Pfosten ausgebildet. Für die Ingenieure ist dies gestalterisch begründet, weil sich eine Ausfachung ohne Pfosten flexibler ausrichten lässt, auch wenn die Knotenpunkte in unregelmässigen Abständen angeordnet sind. Die Ansicht erscheint harmonischer rhythmisiert und letztlich auch eleganter. Ausserdem entfällt der Kehrpunkt der fallenden Diagonalen, da die Zickzacklinie in einem Schwung über die ganze Trägerlänge durchgezogen werden kann. Sämtliche Hohlprofilknoten sind mit voll durchgeschweissten HV-Nähten ausgeführt, Kehlnähte sind für die Verbindung der Hohlprofile nicht zulässig.

Das Fachwerk im Boden, in der Decke und im Dach ist als K-Fachwerk ausgebildet. Die Konstruktion wird dadurch weniger steif, und Zwängungen lassen sich verhindern, weil das Fachwerk «atmen» kann. Die neben den Normalkräften entstehenden Biegebeanspruchungen der Querpfosten sind nicht substanziell und damit vernachlässigbar. Die Funktion als Fachwerk, dessen statische Elemente rechnerisch nur auf Zug und Druck beansprucht werden, bleibt bewahrt.

Der Leichtbau aus Stahl und das aufgelöste Tragwerk als Fachwerk helfen, die neue Brücke an den Bestand zu fügen. Allerdings entstehen mit dem geringen Gewicht auch Schwingungen, die statisch geklärt werden mussten. Dabei waren die vertikalen Schwingungen massgebend. Das galt nicht für den doppelgeschossigen Kastenträger, denn dieser ist wegen seiner Höhe sehr steif. Die eingeschossigen Kastenträger haben allerdings eine Eigenfrequenz im Bereich von ca. 4.0 Hertz, womit die Richtwerte gemäss SIA 260 knapp nicht eingehalten sind. Die dynamische Berechnung berücksichtigte aber nicht die Deckenscheiben in Verbundbauweise, die zusätzlich versteifend wirken. Im Bereich der Hauptspannweite waren provisorisch Schwingungstilger eingeplant, für den Fall, dass eine unerwünschte dynamische Anregung durch Nutzer entstanden wäre. Ihre Installation war auf der Unterseite der Passerelle vorgesehen, wurde jedoch nicht notwendig.

In Querrichtung ist die Brücke relativ schmal und daher schlank und weich. Zudem bietet sie eine grosse Angriffsfläche für den Wind. Das macht die Einwirkung von Wind in horizontaler Richtung zum massgebenden Gefährdungsbild. Die rechnerischen

the view of the box girder, the trusses are developed as pure strut trusses without posts. The engineers justify this as a design issue, in that a bracing without posts can be positioned more flexibly, even when nodes are arranged at irregular intervals. The view appears more harmoniously rhythmic and ultimately also more elegant. Moreover, there is no reversal point of the falling diagonals as the zigzag line can be carried through in a sweep across the entire length of the carrier. All of the hollow profile nodes are carried out with fully through-welded bevel groove welds; fillet welds are not permitted for the connection of the hollow sections.

On the floor, in the ceiling, and on the roof, the truss is developed as K-bracing. The construction is thereby less stiff, and restraints can be avoided because the truss is able to "breathe." The bending stresses in addition to the normal force of the cross posts are not substantial and therefore negligible. The function as a truss whose static elements, by way of calculation, have only tensile and compressive stresses remains preserved.

The lightweight construction made of steel and the dispersed supporting structure as truss help the new bridges join together with the existing structures. Nevertheless, because of the low weight, vibrations arise, which had to be statically resolved. Here, the vertical vibrations were decisive. This did not apply to the double-story box girder, as this is very stiff due to its height. The single-story box girders, however, have a natural frequency in the area of ca. 4.0 hertz, whereby the guideline according to SIA 260 is narrowly missed. However, the dynamic calculation does not account for the ceiling disc in composite construction, which has an additional bracing effect. In the area of the main span, provisional vibration absorbers were planned, in the event that an undesirable dynamic stimulation through users should arise. The plan was to install it on the underside of the aerial walkway; however, this was not necessary.

The bridge is relatively narrow in the cross direction and therefore slender and soft. Furthermore, it offers a large surface for the wind. That makes the impact of wind in a horizontal direction the crucial hazard scenario. The calculated natural frequencies in a horizontal direction are in the range of more than 1.3 hertz, in this case thus complying with the guideline according to SIA 260, table 10.

SKILLED MONTAGE WITHOUT FALSEWORK

In summer 2017 the prefabricated steel construction was delivered in six component parts and welded together on the installation

Eigenfrequenzen in horizontaler Richtung liegen im Bereich von über 1.3 Hertz. In diesem Fall sind somit die Richtwerte gemäss SIA 260, Tabelle 10, eingehalten.

GESCHICKTE MONTAGE OHNE LEERGERÜST

Im Sommer 2017 wurde die vorfabrizierte Stahlbaukonstruktion in sechs Bauteilen angeliefert und vor Ort auf dem Installationsplatz beim Parkhaus zusammengeschweisst. Da die Lindenstrasse und das Parking Böschenmühle, mit Ausnahme einer Tagessperrung, über die gesamte Bauzeit befahrbar sein sollten, war es nicht möglich, ein Leergerüst zu stellen. Die untere Ebene des Haupttragwerks wurde deshalb in einem Stück eingehoben und danach die obere Ebene darauf montiert. Auf diese Weise funktionierte die untere Ebene als Leergerüst für die darüberliegende Konstruktion. Die Montage aller Segmente konnte dadurch innerhalb eines Arbeitstags erfolgen.

Nach der Montage wurde der Stahlbau rundum mit Sandwichelementen verkleidet. Das gegen Korrosion beschichtete Tragwerk liegt somit auf der witterungsgeschützten Innenseite, wo es sichtbar belassen ist und die Korridore rhythmisiert. Es distanziert sich durchaus vom kühlen und klinischen Erscheinungsbild, das oft in Spitälern herrscht.

Die Böden sind als Stahlbetonverbunddecken ausgebildet, die Flachdächer bestehen aus einer Trapezblecheindeckung mit einem Flachdachaufbau. Von aussen erscheint die Brücke im städtischen Konglomerat als kompaktes Volumen mit einer minimal strukturierten Oberfläche. Einzig kleine rechteckige Fensteröffnungen, die mehr Gucklöchern gleichen, gliedern die Fläche ruhig und unaufgeregt. Eine durchaus funktional begründete Gestaltung: Der Patientenbereich bleibt blickdicht, Besucher können dennoch punktuelle Eindrücke aus der Umgebung erhaschen.

ZWECKGEBUNDEN GESTALTET

Für einen Standort mit einer derart komplexen Situation, die sich während der Bauphase noch wandelte, ist es für die Planenden eine Herausforderung, eine angemessene und allenfalls gar selbstverständliche Lösung zu finden. Dass dies durchaus möglich ist, demonstriert die Passerelle auf überraschend pragmatische Art. Die neue Verbindung über die Lindenstrasse ist in erster Linie funktional, bettet sich aber gekonnt in den gegebenen korsettartigen Kontext ein. Sie ist in diesem Sinne kein auffallendes Kolorit in der Umgebung – soll sie auch nicht sein –, sondern vielmehr ein zurückhaltender sowie durchdacht, griffig und angemessen gestalteter Zweckbau.

site near the parking garage. Since Lindenstrasse and the Böschenmühle parking area were accessible during the entire building period, with the exception of a one-day closure, it was not possible to put up falsework. The lower level of the main supporting structure was therefore lifted in, in one piece, and the upper levels were subsequently mounted on top of it. Thus, the lower level worked as falsework for the construction on top of it. In this way, only one workday was required for the installation of all segments.

After the installation, the steel structure was clad all around with sandwich elements. The supporting structure, with an anticorrosion coating, thereby lies on the weather-protected inside, where it is left visible and gives a rhythm to the corridor. It thoroughly distances itself from the cool and clinical appearance that often dominates in hospitals.

The floors are developed as reinforced steel composite floors and the flat roofs are made up of a trapezoidal sheet metal covering with a flat roof construction. From outside, the bridge appears within the urban conglomerate as a compact volume with a minimally structured surface. Only small, right-angled window openings resembling peepholes calmly and unexcitedly organize the surface. An entirely functionally well-founded design: the patient area remains opaque, but visitors can nonetheless sneak sporadic impressions of the surroundings.

DESIGNED FOR A PURPOSE

For a location with such a complex situation that was still changing during the building phase, it is a challenge for planners to find an appropriate and, at best, even self-evident solution. In a surprising and pragmatic way, the aerial walkway demonstrates that this is entirely possible. While the new connection above Lindenstrasse is, indeed, first and foremost functional, it skillfully embeds itself in the given, corset-like, context. In this sense, it is certainly not a flamboyant dash of color in the surroundings—and it is not meant to be—but instead is a modest functional building with a sophisticated, succinct, and suitable design.

Haus 10, Passerelle / Building 10, aerial walkway
Fotos / Photos: Georg Aerni

DAS ZEN DES STAHLS
Fawad Kazi, James Licini, Marko Sauer

THE ZEN OF STEEL
Fawad Kazi, James Licini, Marko Sauer

«Nur ein ganz kleiner teil der architektur gehört der kunst an: Das grabmal und das denkmal. Alles andere, alles, was einem zweck dient, ist aus dem reiche der kunst auszuschließen. [...] Das haus hat allen zu gefallen. Zum unterschiede vom kunstwerk, das niemandem zu gefallen hat. Das kunstwerk ist eine privatangelegenheit des künstlers. Das haus ist es nicht.»

Adolf Loos, «Ornament und Verbrechen» (1908), in: *Trotzdem.* 1900–1930, hg. von Adolf Opel, Wien 1982 (Innsbruck 1931), S. 78

Only a tiny part of architecture comes under art: tombs and monuments. Everything else, everything that serves some practical purpose, should be ejected from the realm of art. [...] A building should please everyone, unlike a work of art, which does not have to please anyone. A work of art is a private matter for the artist, a building is not.

Adolf Loos, "Architecture," *Neue Freie Presse,* Vienna 1910

Haus 10, Netzersatzanlage, Stahlverband zur Stabilisierung des Gebäudes gegen Erdbeben / Building 10, emergency power system, steel lattice to stabilize the building against earthquakes
Foto / Photo: Florian Brunner

James Licini nimmt sich Zeit, um den Pavillon in Ruhe zu studieren. Akribisch analysiert sein Blick die Konstruktion, folgt den Lasten auf ihrem Weg in den Boden, untersucht, wie die Träger untereinander im System wirken. Um den Stahlplastiker und ehemaligen Schlosser herum drängen sich an diesem Freitag die Arbeiter der Baustelle, die Maschinen stampfen in der riesigen Baugrube, in der dereinst die Tiefgarage unterkommen wird, und die Kittel der Ärztinnen und Ärzte blähen sich auf, wenn sie an der kleinen Gruppe vorbeieilen, die als einzige in diesem geschäftigen Getümmel unbeweglich verharrt.

Eine Begehung des Stahlbauers und Künstlers James Licini mit dem Architekten Fawad Kazi und dem Herausgeber Marko Sauer führt zu vier Stationen in diesem Grossprojekt, an denen Metall als Baustoff eine entscheidende Rolle spielt: zum Pavillon des Restaurants, zur Passerelle als Verbindungsstück zum Haus 10 sowie zu dessen Treppenhaus und Fassade. Seit vielen Jahren verbindet Kazi und Licini eine Freundschaft, und sie pflegen einen regen Austausch über ihre Disziplinen und Motive. Was lässt sich bezüglich des Stahlbaus von einem Künstler lernen, dessen Hände ein Leben lang in Berührung mit dem Material standen und der als präziser Handwerker und feinnerviger Gestalter dem Stahl zu einer freieren Form verhalf?

Licini gilt als Vertreter der konkreten Kunst, und er arbeitet ausschliesslich mit den industriell gefertigten Elementen aus dem Standardsortiment des Stahlbaus: Träger, Winkeleisen und Stahlplatten. In dieser Materialwahl spiegelt sich die Vita des 1937 geborenen Licini, der als gelernter Schlosser auf dem Bau arbeitete, bevor er 1968 seine ersten Stahlplastiken erstellte. Diese beruhen immer auf der ursprünglichen Form und Beschaffenheit des verwendeten Materials, Licini arrangiert und verbindet die Stahlträger zu Skulpturen in den unterschiedlichsten Massstäben. Die Präzision der Machart, der materialgerechte Einsatz des Stahls und die daraus resultierende Wirkung stehen für ihn im Vordergrund. Diese Präzision vermisst er oft bei

James Licini takes his time, studies the pavilion calmly. His gaze analyzes the construction meticulously, follows the loads on their way into the ground, examines how the supports work together in the system. Workers at the construction site crowd around the steel sculptor and former metalworker on this Friday as they pound machines into the huge excavation pit where the underground parking garage will be housed; doctors with their white gowns billowing rush by the small group, the only ones standing still in this hustle and bustle.

The steelworker and artist James Licini, architect Fawad Kazi, and publisher Marko Sauer are on an inspection leading them to four stations in this major project in which metal plays a decisive role as building material. Their tour takes them to the restaurant pavilion, the aerial walkway as connecting element to Building 10, its stairway, and its façade. Kazi and Licini, who have been friends for years, maintain an active discussion about their disciplines and motives. What is there to learn about steel construction from an artist whose hands have spent a lifetime in contact with the material and who, as a precise artisan and delicate designer, helps bring steel to a freer form?

Licini, considered a representative of concrete art, works exclusively with industrially prepared elements from the standard range of steel construction: beams, angle irons, and steel plates. This choice of materials reflects the life of the artist, who was born in 1937. As a trained metalworker, he worked in construction until producing his first steel sculpture in 1968. His sculptures always comprise the original form and qualities of the material used. Licini arranges and connects the steel supports to sculptures in various dimensions. At the forefront for him are the precision of the design, the use of steel in a way appropriate to the material, and the resulting effect. He finds that architecture often lacks this precision: "A lot is kitsch and overloaded with details. What bothers me most is the diversion of materials from their intended use, as often occurs with chromium steel pipes and steel cables."

der Architektur: «Vieles ist Kitsch und mit Details überfrachtet. Am meisten stört mich der zweckentfremdete Einsatz des Materials, wie er sich häufig in Chromstahlrohren und Drahtseilen ausdrückt.»

KANTINE – DAS ZWECKMÄSSIGE

Der Pavillon zwischen Haus 03 und Haus 04 war der erste Baustein des Grossprojekts KSSG–OKS. Das kleine Gebäude birgt in seinem Untergeschoss eine Trafostation und die beiden betonierten Kamine stossen als knapp zweigeschossige Türme an die Oberfläche. Auf ihnen liegt ein Rost aus Stahlprofilen, der das eigentliche Dach bildet. Wie beginnt Licini seine Analyse des Gebäudes? «Wenn ich ein Gebäude betrachte, dann stört mich etwas – oder es stört mich nichts. Wenn mich nichts stört, dann hat die Konstruktion eine Selbstverständlichkeit. Wenn man sich an die Empfehlungen des Ingenieurs hält, dann ist man schon mal weg vom Kitsch und landet beim Zweckgebundenen. Denn was zweckgebunden ist, ist auch selbstverständlich. Sobald ich etwas als störend empfinde, dann fange ich an, genauer zu schauen und zu suchen, was es denn ist, das stört.»

Die Kantine besteht diesen ersten Test, und Licini kommentiert die plastisch geformte Konsole am Betonkern, auf der das gesamte Dach aufliegt. Er arbeitet sich durch die ganze Konstruktion und scheint sie mit seinen Augen zu sezieren. «Da bleibe ich nirgends hängen. Das ist sehr zweckgebunden», lautet das Fazit nach eingehender Begutachtung. Am Übergang vom Dach des Pavillons zum Bestand hält Licini jedoch inne und nimmt ein Bauteil genauer ins Visier. «Das ist interessant. Dieses Profil kann ich mir nicht erklären. Ich weiss nicht, welche Funktion es übernimmt.» Kazi bestätigt, dass es sich an dieser Stelle um eine bewusste Ausnahme im System handelt. Das Dach des Pavillons sollte statisch vom Bestand getrennt werden und ein unabhängiges Bauteil bleiben. Deshalb schliesst der Gitterrost mit einem dickwandigen Vierkantprofil, das die Konstruktion vollendet. Licini entdeckt an selber Stelle einen Wechsel in der Tragweise. «Das ist raffiniert: Der Träger wird zur Konsole und trägt hinter der Verschraubung. Er bekommt dadurch eine Leichtigkeit. Mit der Verschraubung erfüllt er zwar immer noch die statische Funktion des Trägers, aber er wirkt als Konsole. Doch das Geheimnis ist dieses dickwandige Profil, das alles zusammenhält.» Trotz aller Zweckmässigkeit, die dem Pavillon innewohnt, lässt sich in dieser kühnen Geste eine Brücke zu den Werken von Licini schlagen. Und auch die enormen Schrauben, die den Rost zusammenhalten, wecken seine Aufmerksamkeit. «Diese

RESTAURANT — FUNCTIONALITY

The pavilion between Building 03 and Building 04 was the first building block of the major KSSG–OKS project. The small structure conceals a transfer station in its basement, and two cemented chimneys meet the surface as scant two-story towers. On them is a grid of steel sections, which forms the actual roof. How does Licini begin his analysis of the building? "When I view a building, then either something disturbs me, or nothing does. When nothing disturbs me, then the construction has a self-evidence. When you abide by the engineer's suggestions, then you've already moved away from kitsch, and you arrive at something earmarked for a specific purpose. Things that are earmarked for a purpose are also self-evident. As soon as I sense something that disturbs me, then I begin to look closer and search for what it is that causes the disturbance."

The restaurant passes this first test, and Licini comments on the sculptural console on the concrete core, which supports the entire roof. He works through the whole construction and seems to dissect it with his eye. "I don't get stuck anywhere here. This is very functional," is his conclusion after a thorough assessment. On the transition from the roof of the pavilion to the existing buildings, however, Licini pauses and concentrates more closely on one section of the building. "That's interesting. I can't explain this profile. I don't know what function it has." At this point, Kazi confirms that it is a deliberate exception in the system. The roof of the pavilion is meant to be separated statically from the existing buildings and remain an independent structural element. That's why the grating finishes with a thick-walled square profile that completes the construction. At the same point, Licini discovers a change in the load-bearing method. "That's ingenious: the carrier becomes a console and bears the load behind the screw connection. In that way, it attains a lightness. It still fulfills the carrier's static function with the screw connection, yet looks like a console. But the secret is this thick-walled profile that holds everything together." Despite all the practicality inherent in the pavilion, this clever gesture creates a bridge to Licini's works. And the enormous screws that hold the grate together also catch his attention. "The engineer dimensioned these screws based on tensile and shearing forces. That all has to fit together — also the holes, then everything is practical. That's part of the self-conception. This function has to be fulfilled, otherwise a lot of other measures would be necessary to compensate for it. And if so, in the end, it would then be no longer practical again."

Fawad Kazi und James Licini im Pavillon, 03.07.2020 / Fawad Kazi and James Licini in the pavilion, July 3, 2020
Fotos / Photos: Daniel Ammann

Haus 10, Ansicht West / Building 10, view to the west
Foto / Photo: Georg Aerni

Schrauben hat der Ingenieur auf Zug und Scherkräfte dimensioniert. Das muss alles zusammenpassen – auch die Löcher, dann ist alles zweckmässig. Das ist Teil des Selbstverständnisses. Diese Funktion muss erfüllt sein, denn sonst braucht es wieder ganz viele andere Massnahmen, um das zu kompensieren. Und am Ende ist es dann wiederum nicht mehr zweckmässig.»

PASSERELLE – DER ZEN-MOMENT

Der Weg führt weiter zur Passerelle, die das Haus 10 mit dem Spitalareal verbindet. Gleich nachdem sich die Schiebetüren am südlichen Ende hinter der Gruppe geschlossen haben, äussert sich James Licini mit Erstaunen: «Die Passerelle ist zwar neu, sie sieht aber aus, als ob sie schon immer da gewesen wäre.» Er führt dies zurück auf die Ehrlichkeit der Konstruktion, auf die Direktheit der Umsetzung, bei der so lange reduziert wurde, bis man nichts mehr wegnehmen konnte. Das verleiht der Konstruktion etwas Zeitloses und Gültiges. Die Passerelle ist in erster Linie ein Ingenieurbauwerk, das seine Funktion unter sehr eng gefassten Rahmenbedingungen erfüllen muss. Der Spielraum für die Gestaltung war hier minimal. Und dennoch erfährt die Begehung genau an diesem Ort einen eindrücklichen Moment.

An der Stelle, wo sich die beiden Wege innerhalb der Passerelle trennen, hält Licini plötzlich inne und geht ein paar Schritte zurück, dann wieder einige vor. Sein Blick richtet sich auf ein Stützenpaar, das sich an der Gabelung der Wege befindet. «Der Stahlbauer hat hier hervorragende Arbeit geleistet», kommentiert er schliesslich seine Beobachtungen. «Man muss den Spalt zwischen diesen Stützen anschauen. Ein Millimeter, maximal zwei Millimeter. Man konzentriert sich beim Vorbeilaufen nur auf diesen Spalt, man läuft weiter und sieht, wie sich der Spalt kontinuierlich schliesst. Man kann an dieser Stelle sehr gut sehen, wie ausserordentlich präzise dies gemacht wurde. Darin liegt für mich der Zen-Begriff. Ich geniesse diese Genauigkeit. Und ich habe durch diese kleine Beobachtung ein ganz anderes Raumerlebnis. Bei mir kommt es genau auf diese Dinge an. Das ist das erste, worauf ich achte, wenn ich einen Raum betrete. Wenn das alles passt, dann ist dies für mich ein Hochgenuss.»

TREPPENHAUS – HANDFREUNDLICH

Das kleine Grüppchen lässt die Passerelle hinter sich und betritt das Haus 10 auf der Ebene 4. Das Haus bietet in der Lobby vor den Liften einen Empfang, doch die Route führt direkt weiter in das Haupttreppenhaus. Geschliffene Betonböden verströmen eine gediegene und hochwertige Eleganz, die Aufmerksamkeit

AERIAL WALKWAY — THE ZEN MOMENT

The way leads further to the aerial walkway connecting Building 10 with the hospital grounds. As soon as the sliding doors at the southern end have closed behind the group, Licini exclaims in amazement: "The aerial walkway is new, but it looks like it has always been here." He attributes this to the honesty of the construction, the directness of the realization, which has been minimized to such an extent that there is no longer anything that can be taken away from it. This lends the construction a certain timelessness and validity. The aerial walkway is, first and foremost, an engineering structure that must fulfill its function under very strict framework conditions. Here, the design had minimal leeway. And nonetheless, precisely at this site, the inspection group experiences a powerful moment.

At this point, where the two routes separate within the aerial walkway, Licini pauses and takes a few steps back, then a few forward again. His gaze turns to a pair of supports where the routes part ways. In the end, he comments on what he has observed: "The steel constructor did outstanding work here. You have to look at the gap between these supports. One millimeter, two millimeters maximum. Walking by, you concentrate on this gap alone, you walk on and watch as the gap steadily closes. At this point, you can clearly see the extraordinary precision with which it was made. For me, the concept of Zen is in that. I enjoy this precision. And through this small observation, I have an entirely different spatial experience. For me, it's about precisely these things. When I enter a space, that's what I pay attention to first. When that all fits, it's a special treat for me."

STAIRCASE — HAND-FRIENDLY

The small group moves past the aerial walkway and enters Building 10 on the fourth floor. The building has a reception in the lobby in front of the lifts, but the route leads directly onward to the main stairway. While polished concrete floors radiate a tasteful and sophisticated elegance, attention is on the stake railing that finishes the stairway. Licini lets his hand glide over the construction. His movement falters and his eyes narrow, nearly closing. Finally, he comments dryly, "you had less luck with the metalworker than you with the steel constructor." Licini points to the wavy sections that one feels when sweeping across the handrail. "I am allowed to be critical, because I could do it better myself," says the former building fitter as he calls into play a term that summarizes the quality of a construction. "A work has to be hand-friendly. We used this concept frequently in the past. It

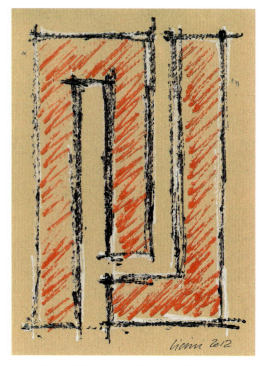

James Licini, Zeichnung, 2012 / James Licini, drawing, 2012
Foto / Photo: Fawad Kazi

Haus 10 und Passerelle, Ansicht Süd / Building 10 and aerial walkway, view to the south
Foto / Photo: Georg Aerni

jedoch gilt den Staketengeländern, die die Treppen abschliessen. Licini lässt die Hand über die Konstruktion gleiten. Er stockt in seiner Bewegung, seine Augen formen sich zu Schlitzen und schliesslich kommentiert er trocken: «Mit dem Schlosser hattet ihr weniger Glück als mit dem Stahlbauer.» Licini weist auf die welligen Stellen hin, die man spürt, wenn man über den Handlauf streicht. «Ich darf das kritisieren, weil ich das besser machen würde», meint der einstige Bauschlosser und bringt einen Begriff ins Spiel, der die Qualität einer Konstruktion auf den Punkt bringt. «Eine Arbeit muss handfreundlich sein. Wir haben diesen Begriff früher oft verwendet. Er beschreibt, wie ein Blinder ein Gebäude wahrnehmen würde. Er kann es zwar nicht mit den Augen sehen, aber er kann es spüren. Seine Hand merkt ganz genau, ob alles richtig ist. Diese Wahrnehmung kann oft präziser sein als das Auge. Man kann optisch etwas machen, was einen zum Anfassen animiert, aber das heisst noch lange nicht, dass es handfreundlich ist.» Diese Handfreundlichkeit fasst in einem Begriff zusammen, was ein Gebrauchsgegenstand alles leisten muss: Er soll sich von Weitem in seiner Erscheinung in den Raum einfügen und ebenso bei der Berührung ein Gefühl der Selbstverständlichkeit auslösen. Dies trifft auf die Tür- und Fenstergriffe zu, die Kazi für das Projekt KSSG–OKS entworfen hat. Die Beschlagslinie, die in der Auseinandersetzung mit der Bauaufgabe entstanden ist, bietet diese haptischen Qualitäten mit einem sich verbreiternden Griff aus fein geschliffenem Chromstahl, der sich gleichsam von selbst in die Hand legt.

FASSADE – GRUPPE UND SERIE

Das Treppenhaus führt zur letzten Station des Rundgangs. An der Steinachstrasse zeigt sich das Haus 10 in seinen sechs Stockwerken und einer streng aufgebauten Fassade. Die Verkleidung aus eloxiertem Aluminium führt in den Brüstungen unter den Fensterreihen als Band rund um das Gebäude, zwischen den einzelnen Fenstern streben lisenenartige Elemente in die Höhe. Licini nimmt sich wieder viel Zeit, um die Ordnung dieser Fassade zu lesen. Und wie aus dieser Ordnung ein neuer Zusammenhang entsteht. «Interessant ist der Wechsel, wenn man fokussiert und wenn man den Blick schweifen lässt. Denn das serielle Prinzip vermag trotz der einfachen Grundidee eine Vielfalt zu erzeugen. Während man die Fassade aus der Nähe und aus einem spitzen Winkel als perforierte Wand wahrnimmt, kippt sie weiter hinten zur Fläche und schliesslich zur Linie.» Und auch wenn bei dieser Fassade gemäss Licini die Grenze zwischen dem Zweckmässigen und der Gestaltung überschritten wird, so findet

describes how blind people perceive a building. They cannot see it with their eyes, but they can feel it. Their hands sense exactly whether everything is right or not. This perception can often be more precise than that of the eye. You can make something that visually animates you to touch it, but in no way does that mean that it is hand-friendly." This hand-friendliness or optimization for the hand summarizes everything a use object has to do: from far away, it should merge with a space in terms of appearance and also trigger a sense of self-evidence when touched. The door and window handles that Kazi designed for the KSSG–OKS project do precisely this. The line of fittings, which arose in a dialogue with the building task, offers these haptic qualities with a broadening grip of finely polished chromatic steel, which places itself in one's hand, as it were.

FAÇADE — GROUP AND SERIES

The stairway leads to the final station of the inspection. Visible at Steinachstrasse is Building 10 with its six floors and strictly developed façade. The cladding of anodized aluminum leads into the railing under the row of windows as a ribbon around the building, pilaster-like elements rise up high between the individual windows. Licini again takes a great deal of time to read the order of this façade and how a new context arises from this arrangement. "What is interesting is the change, when you focus, and when you let your gaze glide across. The serial principle, despite the simple basic idea, is capable of generating diversity. Whereas from up close and from a sharp angle you perceive the façade as a perforated wall, further back it tips to a surface and finally to a line." And even though this façade has crossed the border between functionality and design, according to Licini, he finds a successful relationship between the individual parts and the whole: "When you view a group of individual elements separately, then the group has validity in and of itself, just like with repetition." Licini deconstructs the façade in his mind's eye and examines it for conclusiveness. "With this building, when you multiply the individual groups and develop the façades with such similar elements, then the overall form is valid again. The individual element, in and of itself, is just as conclusive as the form that arises from the repetition and the series. I pay attention to such things. When the whole is not divisible, the possibilities are limited. Divisibility, on the contrary, allows for a freer design of the volume, because also the basic element is valid in and of itself."

During the inspection, Licini comments on various aspects of the metal construction. His comments range from structural

Haus 10, Nebentreppenhaus / Building 10, secondary stairway
Foto / Photo: Georg Aerni

er eine geglückte Beziehung zwischen dem Einzelteil und dem Ganzen: «Wenn man eine Gruppe von einzelnen Elementen gesondert betrachtet, dann hat sie in sich selbst ebenso eine Gültigkeit wie in der Repetition.» Vor seinem geistigen Auge dekonstruiert Licini die Fassade und untersucht sie auf ihre Schlüssigkeit. «Wenn man bei diesem Gebäude die einzelne Gruppe vervielfacht und die Fassade mit solch gleichartigen Elementen aufbaut, dann ist auch die Gesamtform wieder gültig. Das einzelne Element ist für sich genommen ebenso schlüssig wie die Form, die sich aus der Wiederholung und der Serie ergibt. Ich achte auf solche Dinge. Wenn das Gesamte nicht einteilbar ist, schränkt es die Möglichkeiten ein. Eine Unterteilbarkeit dagegen ermöglicht eine freiere Gestaltung des Volumens, weil auch das Grundelement in sich gültig ist.»

James Licini kommentiert auf dem Rundgang verschiedene Aspekte des Metallbaus. Diese reichen von konstruktiven Überlegungen über die handwerkliche Machart bis hin zur Abhängigkeit von Tektonik, Repetition und volumetrischer Erscheinung. So präzise seine Beobachtungen sind, so sehr versucht er, sie zu relativieren. «Ich bin nicht architektonisch gebildet und kann nur aus meiner Betrachtungsweise sprechen. Ich kann keine Architekturkritik machen. Das ist nur meine Analyse dessen, was der Architekt erstellt hat.» Und dennoch bringt er zum Schluss wieder seine ganz persönliche Erfahrung ein, als er sich an Fawad Kazi wendet. «Mich nimmt wunder, was du sagst, wenn du in zwanzig Jahren wieder hier stehst. Was würdest du anders machen? In zwanzig Jahren genügen dir deine Ansprüche wohl nicht mehr mit dem Wissen, das du dann haben wirst. Im Moment ist das gültig. Doch das Gültige verändert sich.»

considerations of the craftsmanship through to dependencies of tectonics, repetition, and volumetric appearance. His observations are extremely precise, and he is equally precise in his attempts to make them relative. "I don't have an architectural education and can only speak from my own point of view. I can't offer any architectural critique. This is simply my analysis of what the architect has created." Nonetheless, in the end he brings in his own personal experience again when he turns to Kazi. "I wonder what you'll say standing here again in twenty years. What would you have done differently? In twenty years, with the knowledge that you'll have, you probably won't be satisfied by your standards anymore. At the moment it's valid. Yet, what's valid, that changes."

James Licini und Fawad Kazi in der Passerelle, 03.07.2020 / James Licini and Fawad Kazi in the aerial walkway, July 3, 2020
Fotos / Photos: Daniel Ammann

DOKUMENTATION HAUS 10
Fawad Kazi

DOCUMENTATION BUILDING 10
Fawad Kazi

S. 53 / p. 53
Situationsplan genordet 1:15'000 /
Site plan, north at top 1:15,000
S. 54 / p. 54
Situationsplan genordet 1:3000 /
Site plan, north at top 1:3000
S. 55 / p. 55
Passerelle und Haus 10, Ansicht Ost /
Aerial walkway and Building 10, view
to the east (Foto / Photo: Georg Aerni)
S. 56 / p. 56
Grundriss Erdgeschoss 1:1500 /
Floor plan, ground floor 1:1500
S. 57 / p. 57
Grundrisse 4. Obergeschoss, 3. Obergeschoss, 1. Obergeschoss, Erdgeschoss 1:500 / Floor plans, 4th floor, 3rd floor, 1st floor, ground floor 1:500
S. 58 / p. 58
Längsschnitt 1:500, Visualisierungen Rohbau und Gebäudetechnik /
Longitudinal section 1:500,
visualizations, shell construction and building technology
S. 59 / p. 59
Querschnitt 1:500, Horizontal- und Vertikalschnitte Fassade 1:35 / Transverse section 1:500, horizontal and vertical sectional view façade 1:35

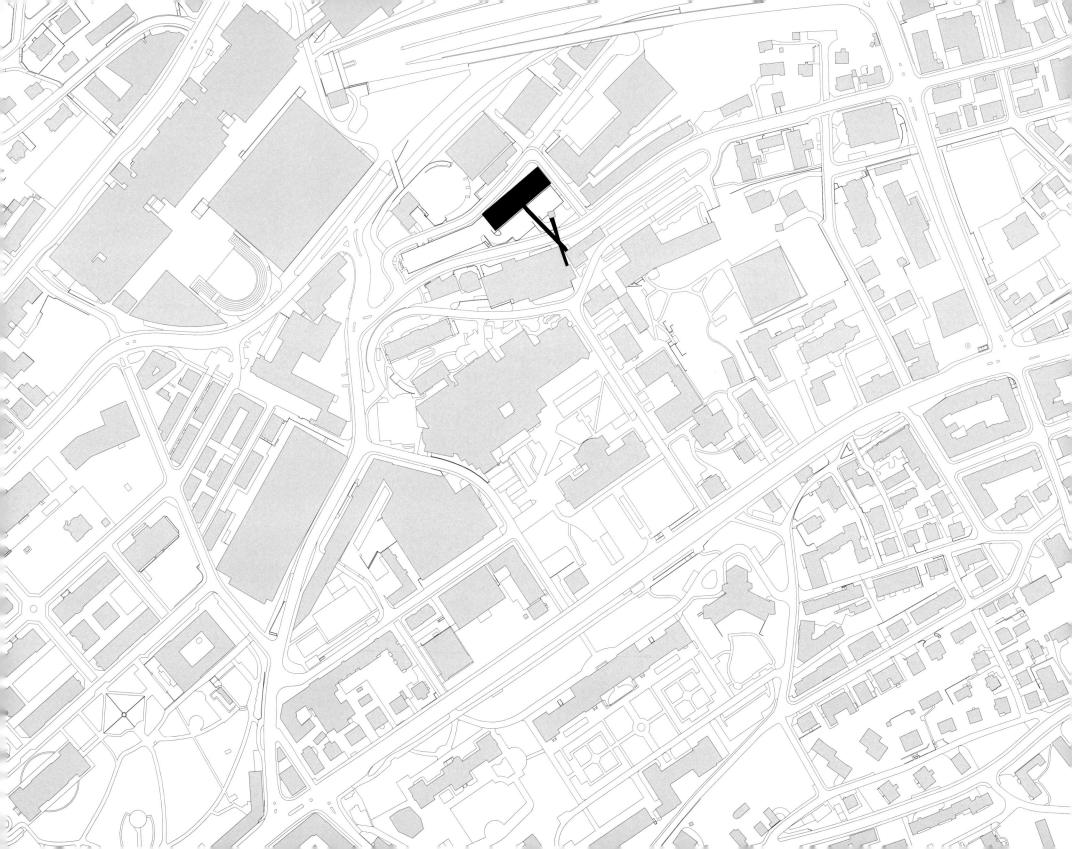

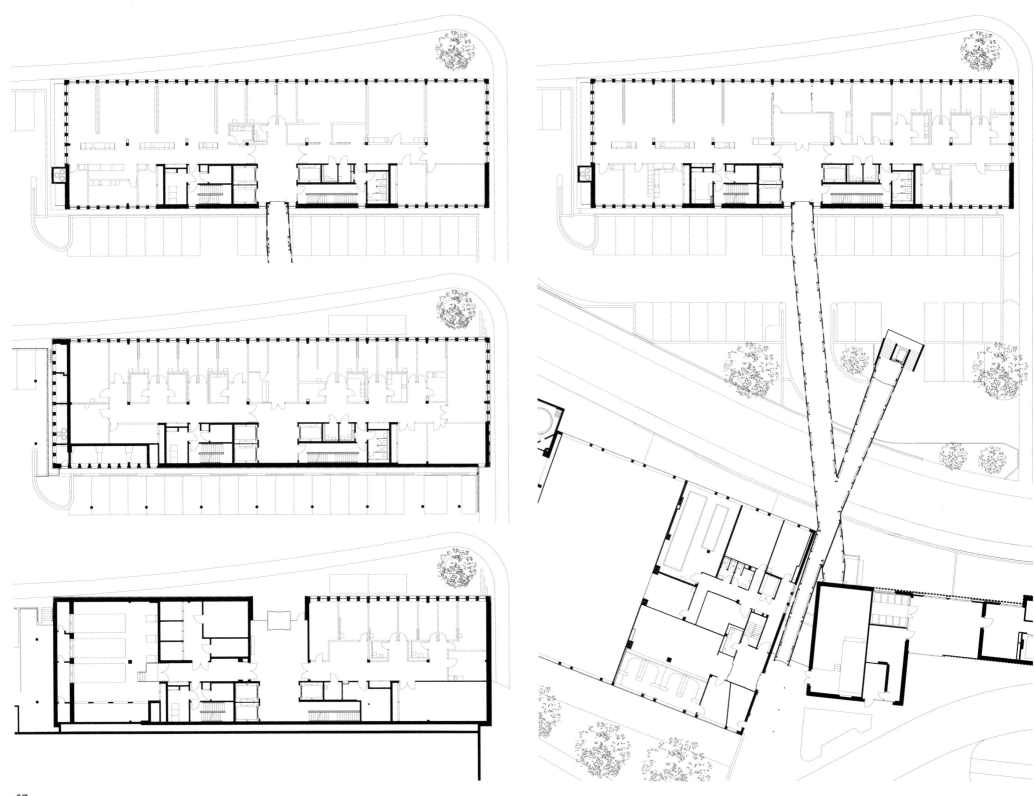

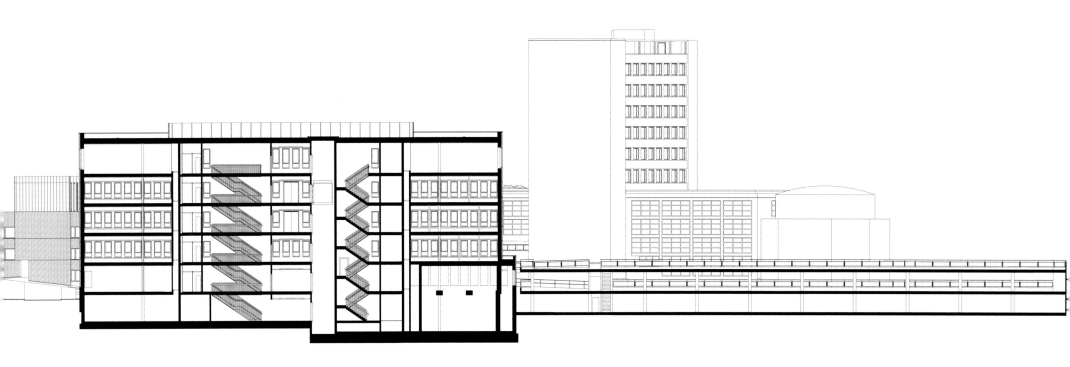

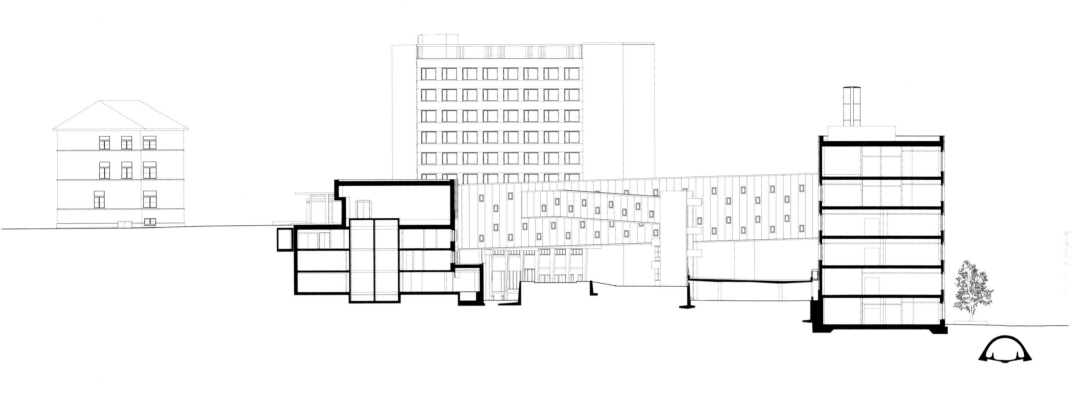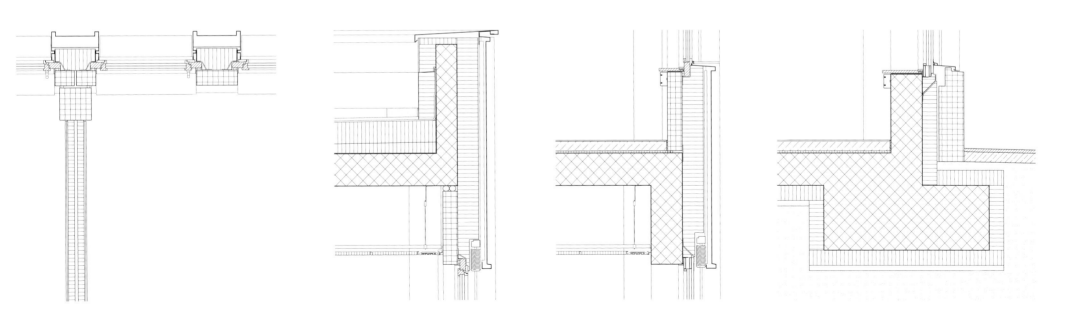

KSSG–OKS

ECKDATEN / KEY DATA

Projektname / Project name
Kantonsspital St.Gallen – Ostschweizer Kinderspital / Cantonal Hospital St.Gallen – Children's Hospital of Eastern Switzerland

Teilprojekte / Subprojects
Kantonsspital St.Gallen / Cantonal Hospital St.Gallen (KSSG)
  Pavillon / Trafostation 2 / Pavilion / Transformer Station 2 (PAV)
  Haus 10 / Building 10 (H10)
  Haus 07A / Building 07A (07A)
  Haus 07B / Building 07B (07B)
Ostschweizer Kinderspital / Children's Hospital of Eastern Switzerland (OKS)

Adresse / Address
Rorschacher Strasse 95, 9007 St.Gallen

Bauherrschaften / Clients
Kanton St.Gallen, Baudepartement / Hochbauamt (bis 2016)
Spitalanlagengesellschaft Kantonsspital St.Gallen
Stiftung Ostschweizer Kinderspital

Auftragnehmer / Contractors
Planergemeinschaft PG KSSG–OKS / Planning group PG KSSG–OKS
Architekt / Architect: Fawad Kazi Architekt GmbH, Zürich
  Projektleitung / Project management: Fawad Kazi (seit / since 2009), Luzius Stiefel (seit / since 2011), Fabian Markel (seit / since 2011), Tommaso Passalacqua (seit / since 2014), Manfred Kunz (seit / since 2015), Hans Kolbeck (seit / since 2020), Britta Fehse (2011–2015), Philipp Macke (2011–2015), Lucius Ueberwasser (2018–2020)
  Teilprojektleitung / Subproject management: Selami Sahin (2013–2014; H10), Stefano Murialdo (2016–2018; H10)

Bauingenieur Tragwerk, Baugrube / Civil engineer for structure, excavation: WaltGalmarini AG, Zürich
  Projektleitung / Project management: Gregorij Meleshko (seit / since 2011), Vincenzo Santoro (seit / since 2014), Andreas Haffter (2014–2018), Oliver Bruckermann (2014–2019)

Ingenieur / Engineer HLKKSE: Amstein + Walthert AG, Zürich
  Projektleitung / Project management: Patrik Stierli (seit / since 2009), David Anderes (seit / since 2011)
  Teilprojektleitung / Subproject management: Andrin Bühlmann (seit / since 2011), Paul Hitz (seit / since 2013), Patrick Schmid (seit / since 2013), Denis Secondo (seit / since 2013), Reto Gasser (seit / since 2018), Rainer Lüber (2011–2016), Peter Winter (2011–2018), Thomas Ledermann (2011–2019), Najra Duranovic (2013–2017)

Subplaner / Subplanner
Projektmanagement / Project management: Hämmerle + Partner GmbH, Zürich
  Projektleitung / Project management: Patrik Hämmerle (seit / since 2009), Matthias Schmid (seit / since 2019), Sabine Hartmutt (2009–2011), Martin Jaschner (2012–2013), Simon Thurnherr (2013–2016), Gwendolin Hohenbleicher (2016–2018)
  Teilprojektleitung / Subproject management: Christian Ernst (seit / since 2015, H4J, PL Stv.), Yvonne Schrank (2013–2015, H4J)

Baumanagement, Bauleitung / Building management, site management: Walter Dietsche Baumanagement AG, Chur
  Projektleitung / Project management: Viktor Ammann (seit / since 2014), Reto Oesch (seit / since 2020), Alfons Zanfrini (2014–2017)
  Bauleitung / Site management: Werner Haas (seit / since 2016), Marco Facchin (seit / since 2017), Alexandre Brandalise (seit / since 2018), Stephan Brunner (seit / since 2020), Cedric Kräutler (seit / since 2020), Marcel Bauer (2016–2018)

Landschaftsarchitektur / Landscape planning: vetschpartner Landschaftsarchitekten AG, Zürich
  Projektleitung / Project management: Nils Lüpke (seit / since 2009), Jürg Zollinger (seit / since 2009), Andreas Klahm (seit / since 2013)

Bauingenieur Werkleitungen, Plätze / Building engineer, works management, squares: BlessHess AG, Luzern
  Projektleitung / Project management: Massimo Sicuranza (seit / since 2016), Samuel Hernandez (2011–2015), Carlo Bless (2011–2019)

Verkehrsplanung / Traffic planning: Enz & Partner GmbH Ingenieurbüro für Verkehrswesen, Zürich
  Projektleitung / Project management: Robert Enz (seit / since 2010)
  Teilprojektleitung / Subproject management: Rudolf Hintermeister (seit / since 2010)

Fassadenplanung / Façade planning: Atelier P3 AG, Zürich
  Projektleitung / Project management: Patrick Valli (seit / since 2018), Martin Gruber (2010–2018)

Lichtplanung / Light planning: Reflexion AG, Zürich
  Projektleitung / Project management: Jonas Godehardt (seit / since 2011), Thomas Mika (seit / since 2016), Daniel Tschudy (2010–2016), Sonja Kägi (2011–2012)

Brandschutz / Fire safety: Amstein + Walthert AG, Zürich
  Projektleitung / Project management: Erich Füglister (seit / since 2010), Stephan Diethelm (seit / since 2011)

Bauphysik, Akustik, Nachhaltigkeit / Structural physics, acoustics, sustainability: Amstein + Walthert AG, Zürich
  Projektleitung / Project management: Marcus Knapp (seit / since 2010), Mario Bleisch (seit / since 2020), Nadège Vetterli (2011–2012), Marc Grossmann (2013–2019)

Sicherheits- / Türfachplanung / Security- / door compartment planning: Amstein + Walthert AG, Zürich
  Projektleitung / Project management: Rita Wiesli (seit / since 2011), Willi Rohner (seit / since 2011)

Kommunikation / Communication ICT: Amstein + Walthert Progress AG, Zürich
  Projektleitung / Project management: Michael Schaffner (seit / since 2011), Peider Felix (2011–2020)

Gebäudeautomation / Building automation: Amstein + Walthert St.Gallen AG, St.Gallen
  Projektleitung / Project management: Hanspeter Keller (seit / since 2012), Franco Baumgartner (seit / since 2012), Marc Dürr (seit / since 2017)

Spital- / Medizinalplanung, Strahlenschutzkonzept / Hospital- / medical planning, radiation protection concept: IBG – Institut für Beratungen im Gesundheitswesen, Aarau
  Projektleitung / project management: Heinrich Messmer (seit / since 2010)

Gastronomieplanung / Gastronomy planning: planbar ag, Zürich
  Projektleitung / Project management: Daniel Mengelt (seit / since 2010)

Signaletik / Signage: Integral Axel Steinberger Zürich GmbH, Zürich
  Projektleitung / Project management: Axel Steinberger (seit / since 2013), Linda Walter (seit / since 2020), Ramona Heiligensetzer (2015–2017)

Weitere Beteiligte / Additional people involved
Masterplan / Master plan: Metron AG, Brugg
Überbauungsplan / Supra-structure plan: ERR Raumplaner AG, St.Gallen
Modelle / Models: Gnädinger Architektur-Modellbau GmbH, St.Gallen (Modelle Bauherrschaften / builder's models)
Visualisierungen / Renderings: Virtual Design Unit GmbH, Zürich (Visualisierungen / Renderings PG KSSG–OKS)

Verfahren / Bidding procedure
Zweistufiger Generalplaner-Projektwettbewerb im selektiven Verfahren nach IVöB / VöB / Two-stage general planning project competition in a selective process according to IVöB/VöB

Termine / Schedule
Wettbewerb (1. und 2. Stufe, Bereinigungsstufe) / Competition (first and second stage, adjustment stage: 2009–2011
Planungsbeginn / Planning start: 2011
Pavillon / Trafostation 2 / Pavilion / Transformer Station 2
  Baubeginn / Construction start: 2016
  Fertigstellung / Completion: 2017
Haus 10 / Building 10
  Baubeginn / Construction start: 2016
  Fertigstellung / Completion: 2018
Haus 07A / Building 07A
  Baubeginn / Construction start: 2018
  Fertigstellung / Completion: 2024
Ostschweizer Kinderspital / Children's Hospital of Eastern Switzerland
  Baubeginn / Construction start: 2020
  Fertigstellung / Completion: 2025
Haus 07B / Building 07B
  Baubeginn / Construction start: 2024
  Fertigstellung / Completion: 2028

PROJEKTBESCHRIEB HAUS 10 / PROJECT DESCRIPTION BUILDING 10

Gebäude / Building
Geschossfläche / Floor area: 6,623.28 m^2
Gebäudevolumen / Building volume: 27,172.00 m^3

Geschosse / Stories
Erdgeschoss / Ground level
1. bis 5. Obergeschoss / 1st to 5th floors

Höhen / Heights
Gebäudehöhe oberirdisch / Building height above ground: 24.99 m
Gebäudehöhe unterirdisch / Building height below ground: 1.20 m
Kaminhöhe / Vent height: 31.32 m
Erdgeschoss / Ground level: 647.70 m ü. M. / m a.s.l.

Passerelle / Aerial walkway
Spannweite / Span width: 50 m
Höhe / Height: 8.70 m
Breite / Width: 3.25 m

Baukosten / Building costs
Gebäude (Haus 10, Netzersatzanlage, Passerelle) / Buildings (Building 10, emergency power system, aerial walkway) SKP 1–9: 35,400,000 CHF, SKP 2: 21,300,000 CHF
Geschossfläche (Quadratmeterpreis) / Floor area (square meter price) SKP 2: 3,211 CHF/m²
Gebäudevolumen (Kubikmeterpreis) / Building volume (cubic meter price) SKP 2: 783 CHF/m³

Nutzungen / Uses
Erdgeschoss / Ground level: Netzersatzanlage, Klinik für Psychosomatik / Emergency power system, clinics for psychosomatics
1. Obergeschoss / 1st floor: Endokrinologie / Diabetologie, Ernährungsberatung / Endocrinology / diabetology, nutrition counseling
2./3. Obergeschoss / 2nd / 3rd floor: Ambulatorium Nephrologie / Hämodialyse / Outpatient clinics for nephrology / hemodialysis
4./5. Obergeschoss / 4th / 5th floor: Ambulatorium Onkologie / Hämatologie / Outpatient clinics for oncology / hematology

Anmerkungen / Notes
Rohbau in Ortbeton / Shell in in-situ concrete
Stützen und Treppenläufe in Fertigbeton / Supports and flights of stairs in precast concrete
Aluminiumfassade / Aluminum façade
Zweigeschossige Passerelle als Stahlfachwerk / Two-story aerial walkway as steel truss construction

Kunst am Bau / Art-in-architecture project
Jean-Christophe De Clercq, Champeix FR
Claudio Moser, Genf

Labels
Keine / None

UNTERNEHMER HAUS 10 /
CONTRACTORS: BUILDING 10

Baugrubenarbeiten / Excavation works:
  KIBAG Bauleistungen AG, St.Gallen
Abbrüche / Demolitions:
  Aemisegger AG, Herisau
Anpassung Betonelemente Haus 24 / Adjustment concrete elements Building 24:
  Loacker AG, Hauptwil
Elektroanschlüsse Monitoring, Starkstrominstallationen / Monitoring of electrical connections, high voltage installations:
  Huber+Monsch AG, St.Gallen
Monitoring / Monitoring:
  ZC Ziegler Consultants AG, Zürich
Geotechnische Begleitung Tiefbauarbeiten / Geotechnical control of underground construction:
  FlumGeo AG, St.Gallen
Baumeisterarbeiten / Master builder work:
  Feldmann Bau AG Bilten, Bilten
Gerüste / Scaffolding:
  Mattiello Gerüstbau AG, Altstätten
Betonkosmetik / Concrete cosmetics:
  DESAX AG, Gommiswald
Maurerarbeiten, Belagsarbeiten / Masonry, surfacing works:
  Implenia Schweiz AG, St.Gallen
Montagebau in Stahl / Industrialized steel construction:
  Schneider Stahlbau AG, Jona
Fassadenbau aus Metall / Metal façade construction:
  Krapf AG, Engelburg
Hochwasserklappschott / Anti-flooding bulkhead:
  JOMOS Brandschutz AG, Balsthal
Mobile Hochwasserschutzwand / Mobile flood protection wall:
  SISTAG AG, Eschenbach
Fenster aus Holz/Metall / Wood/metal windows:
  4B AG, Hochdorf
Bedachungsarbeiten / Roofing work:
  Burkhardt Gebäudehülle AG, Maienfeld
Fugendichtungen / Joint sealing:
  BauDicht AG, St.Gallen
Spezielle Feuchtigkeitsabdichtungen / Special moisture sealing:
  SikaBau AG, St.Gallen
Brandschutzbekleidungen / Fire protection linings:
  Galli + Co. GmbH, Buchs
Lamellenstoren / Venetian blinds:
  Griesser AG, St.Gallen
MS-Hauptverteilungen, Brandmeldeanlage / Medium voltage-main distribution, fire detection system:
  Siemens Schweiz AG, Zürich
Transformatoren, Netzkabel / Transformers, network cables:
  Arnold AG, Fehraltorf
NS-Hauptverteilungen, Unterverteilungen, Sanitäranlagen / Low voltage main distribution, sub-distributions, sanitation:
  Bouygues E&S InTec Schweiz AG, St.Gallen

Netzersatzanlage / Emergency power system:
  Avesco AG, Langenthal
USV-Anlage / Uninterrupted power supply unit:
  GE Consumer & Industrial SA, Riazzino
Gleichstromanlage / Direct current unit:
  Statron AG, Mägenwil
Medienkanäle / Media ducts:
  BRECO-Bauelemente AG, St.Gallen
Leuchten / Lighting:
  MOOS licht ag, Luzern
Patientenrufanlage / Patient calling system:
  Tyco Integrated Fire & Security (Schweiz) AG, Pfäffikon
Schwachstrominstallationen / Low voltage installations:
  cablex AG, Gümligen
Gebäudeautomation / Building automation:
  Sauter Building Control Schweiz AG, Gossau
Erweiterung Notstromsteuerung / Expansion emergency power control:
  Chestonag Automation AG, Seengen
Wärme- und Kälteanlagen / Heating and cooling systems:
  E3 HLK AG, St.Gallen
Lüftungsanlagen / Ventilation system:
  ENGIE Services AG, St.Gallen
Dämmungen HKS / Insulation HKS:
  JADA Isolierungen GmbH, Winterthur
Osmoseanlage, Konzentratmischanlage Hämodialyse / Osmosis unit, concentrate mixing system, hemodialysis:
  Fresenius Kabi (Schweiz) AG, Oberdorf
Gas-, Druckluft-, Vakuumanlage / Gas, pressure, and vacuum systems:
  Dräger Schweiz AG, Liebefeld
Aufzugsanlagen / Elevator systems:
  Schindler Aufzüge AG, St.Gallen
Vorsatzschale Durchgang Passerelle / Facing shell aerial walkway passage:
  Tinella AG, St.Gallen
Gipserarbeiten / Plastering work:
  Kurt Melliger & Söhne AG, Davos Platz
Innentüren aus Metall / Interior metallic doors:
  Oppikofer Stahl- & Metallbau AG, Frauenfeld
Allgemeine Metallbauarbeiten / General metal construction:
  PS Metall AG, Netstal
Metallbauarbeiten Treppengeländer / Metal construction stair railings:
  fehrtech ag, Buchberg
Metallbauarbeiten Klappdeckel NEA / Metal construction hinged lid emergency power system:
  Wibatec AG, Malters
Innentüren aus Holz, Schränke und Einbauküchen / Interior wooden doors, cabinets and fitted kitchens:
  Zomo form AG, Au
Schachtabschlüsse / Shaft connections:
  Heim AG, Waltenswil
Einbaumöbel aus Holz / Built-in wooden furniture:
  Koster AG Holzwelten, Arnegg

Allgemeine Schreinerarbeiten / General carpentry:
  Neue Creaform AG, Krummenau
Glaswände / Glass walls:
  VetroWall AG, Baar
Schliessanlage / Locking system:
  FERROFLEX Owi Sargans AG, Sargans
Elementwände / Element walls:
  Scherrer AG, Bütschwil
Unterlagsböden / Subflooring:
  Pitaro GmbH, Sargans
PU-Kunstharzbelag Passarelle / PU-artificial resin aerial walkway:
  SENN + WIDMER AG, Romanshorn
Bodenbeläge aus Linoleum, Kunststoff und Textilien / Floor covering of linoleum, synthetics, and textiles:
  Daniel Fournier AG, Regensdorf
Bodenbeläge aus Kunststein / Artificial stone floor covering:
  Walo Bertschinger AG, St.Gallen
Boden- und Wandbeläge aus Platten / Panel floor and wall coverings:
  Markus Baumann, Rorschach
Doppelböden / False floors:
  Lenzlinger Söhne AG, Uster
Deckenbekleidungen aus Metall / Metal ceiling linings:
  Röösli AG, Rothenburg
Innere Malerarbeiten / Interior painting:
  T. Ruggiero & Söhne AG, Wil
Oberflächenbehandlungen / Surface treatments:
  Hofmann Malerei AG, St.Gallen
Bauaustrocknung / Drying out of building:
  Krüger + Co. AG, Degersheim
Baureinigung / Building cleaning:
  Fortas AG, St.Gallen
Zutrittskontrollanlage / Access control system:
  dormakaba Holding AG, Rümlang
Rohrpostanlage / Pneumatic post system:
  Aerocom GmbH & Co., St.Gallen
Parkuhren / Parking meters:
  Digitalparking AG, Dietikon
Provisorische Baugespanne / Provisional building marker:
  Keller + Steiner AG, Fahrwangen
Mobiliar / Furnishings:
  Lista Office Ostschweiz, St.Gallen
Baustellensignalisation / Construction site signalization:
  Grafitec AG, St.Gallen

BIOGRAFIEN / BIOGRAPHIES

GEORG AERNI
Geboren 1959, Architekturstudium an der ETH Zürich. 1986–1992 Architekt bei Arnold & Vrendli Amsler in Winterthur. Seit 1994 selbstständig als autodidaktischer Fotograf. Sein künstlerisches Werk bewegt sich an der Schnittstelle von Architektur und Natur, von Stadt und Landschaft. 2011 erschien bei Scheidegger & Spiess seine umfassende Monografie *Sites & Signs*.

Born in 1959, he studied architecture at ETH Zurich; self-taught in photography. From 1986 to 1992 he was employed as an architect at Arnold & Vrendli Amsler, Winterthur. Since 1994, he has worked as a freelance photographer. His artistic photography operates at thresholds between architecture and nature, city and landscape. In 2011, his monograph *Sites & Signs* was published by Scheidegger & Spiess.

FLORIAN BRUNNER
Geboren 1978, Grafiker EFZ und dipl. Gestalter HF, seit 2012 Mitinhaber von Schalter&Walter. Zusätzlich seit 2005 als Fotograf im Bereich Corporate und Architektur tätig. Fotografiert seit über zehn Jahren regelmässig für das Kantonsspital St.Gallen.

Born in 1978, Graphic Designer EFZ (Swiss certification) and Dipl.-Designer HF, co-owner of Schalter&Walter since 2012. Also active as a photographer in the areas of corporate and architectural photography since 2005. He has photographed regularly for the Cantonal Hospital St.Gallen for more than ten years.

LORENZO DE CHIFFRE
Geboren 1974, hat an der Königlich Dänischen Kunstakademie und der University of East London studiert. Mitarbeit und Projektleitung bei Caruso St John Architects in London sowie bei BEHF und Werner Neuwirth in Wien, wo er hauptsächlich an größeren Wohnbauprojekten beteiligt war. Seit 2011 lehrt Lorenzo De Chiffre an der TU Wien. 2016 promovierte er hier zum Wiener Terrassenhaus, 2017 kuratierte er die Ausstellung „Das Terrassenhaus. Ein Wiener Fetisch?" im Architekturzentrum Wien. In seiner Lehre und Forschung befasst sich Lorenzo De Chiffre in erster Linie mit architektonischen Entwurfsstrategien. Zu diesem Thema hat er 2018 das Buch *Ikonen. Methodische Experimente im Umgang mit architektonischen Referenzen* als Mitherausgeber publiziert.

Born in 1974, he studied at the Royal Danish Academy of Fine Arts and at the University of East London. He has worked as a project architect at Caruso St John Architects in London as well as for the architectural firms BEHF and Werner Neuwirth in Vienna, where he was mainly involved in major residential building projects. Lorenzo De Chiffre has taught at the TU Vienna since 2011. Here he also wrote his doctoral thesis on the Viennese-style stepped-section building ("Wiener Terrassenhaus") in 2016 and curated the exhibition "Das Terrassenhaus. Ein Wiener Fetisch?" at Architekturzentrum Wien in 2017. Lorenzo De Chiffre's main interests in teaching and research are architectural design strategies. In 2018, he published and co-edited the book *Ikonen. Methodische Experimente im Umgang mit architektonischen Referenzen*.

CLEMENTINE HEGNER-VAN ROODEN
Geboren 1973, absolvierte ein Bauingenieurstudium an der ETH Zürich und war Assistentin an der Professur für Tragkonstruktionen, Departement Architektur. Fünf Jahre Projektleiterin bei Stocker & Partner in Bern und Zürich. 2006–2013 Redaktorin bei TEC21. Daneben Fachdidaktikerin (Höheres Lehramt ETH). Seit 2013 selbstständige Fachjournalistin, freie Publizistin im Bereich Ingenieurbau, Korrespondentin bei TEC21 und Chefredaktorin der Website für die Gesellschaft für Ingenieurbaukunst.

Born in 1973, she successfully completed civil engineering studies at ETH Zurich and worked as an assistant at the professorship for supporting structures in the Department of Architecture. Project director at Stocker & Partner in Bern and Zurich for five years. From 2006 to 2013, journalist for TEC21; also a content specialist in the Education Department at ETH. Since 2013, a freelance journalist and freelance publicist in the area of civil engineering, correspondent for TEC21 and editor-in-chief of the website for the Gesellschaft für Ingenieurbaukunst (Society for the Art of Civil Engineering).

FAWAD KAZI
Geboren 1971 in London, lebt in Zürich und Wien. Architekturstudium an der ETH Zürich und der Columbia University New York, Diplom 1999 bei Hans Kollhoff. Anschliessend arbeitete er bei Adolf Krischanitz in Wien und unternahm 2001 eine mehrmonatige Orientreise. Seit 2001 eigenes Architekturbüro in Zürich. Wichtige Bauten sind das Schulzentrum Fagen in Bozen (2001–2009), das Gebäude LEE der ETH Zürich (2007–2015) und der Neubauvorhaben für das Kantonsspital St.Gallen und das Ostschweizer Kinderspital (2009–2028). Diverse Ausstellungen, Jurytätigkeiten und Lehraufträge im In- und Ausland.

Born in 1971 in London, he now lives in Zurich and Vienna. Studied architecture at the ETH Zurich and at Columbia University New York, graduated with a diploma in 1999 under Hans Kollhoff. Subsequently worked with Adolf Krischanitz in Vienna and undertook a several-month journey in the Orient in 2001. Since 2001, he has had his own architectural office in Zurich. Important buildings include the school complex Fagen in Bolzano (2001–2009), the LEE Building of the ETH Zurich (2007–2015), and the new building project for the Cantonal Hospital St.Gallen and the Children's Hospital of Eastern Switzerland (2009–2028). Various exhibitions, jury activities, and lectureships internationally.

JAMES LICINI
Geboren 1937 in Zürich, lebt und arbeitet in Hermikon/Dübendorf und Nürensdorf. Ursprünglich Lehre als Schmied in Zürich. 1968 erste Stahlplastiken. In den 1970er-Jahren mehrere Stipendien und ausgedehnte Reisen in die USA, später auch nach Spanien und Mexiko. 1974 eidgenössisches Kunststipendium. Zahlreiche Einzel- und Gruppenausstellungen im In- und Ausland. Viele seiner Werke sind im öffentlichen Raum in der Region Zürich aufgestellt.

Born in Zurich in 1937, lives and works in Hermikon/Dübendorf and Nürensdorf. Originally, a blacksmith apprentice in Zurich. In 1968, Licini created his first steel sculpture. In the 1970s, several grants and extended travel in the United States, later also in Spain and Mexico. In 1974, Licini received the Swiss Art Award. Numerous solo and group exhibitions in Switzerland and abroad. Several of his works are exhibited in Zurich's public space.

BRUNO MARGRETH
Geboren 1973, arbeitet seit 2003 selbstständig als visueller Gestalter im Print-Bereich mit dem Schwerpunkt Editorial Design und Buchgestaltung zwischen Zürich und Berlin. Er hält Vorträge und arbeitet als Lehrbeauftragter an verschiedenen Hochschulen in der Schweiz. Mit seinen Arbeiten gewann er diverse nationale und internationale Auszeichnungen.

Born in 1973, he has worked as a self-employed visual designer in the area of print with a focus on editorial design and book design, in both Zurich and Berlin, since 2003. He gives lectures and works as an assistant professor at various universities in Switzerland. He has won diverse national and international awards with his works.

MARKO SAUER
Geboren 1974, studierte Pädagogik und Architektur. Drei Jahre Projektarchitekt bei Staufer & Hasler, Frauenfeld. Anschliessend Leiter Assistenz im Hochbauamt der Stadt St.Gallen und 2013–2016 Redaktor bei TEC21. Daneben seit 2013 selbstständiger Publizist mit Artikeln in verschiedenen Fachzeitschriften und Tageszeitungen sowie diversen Buchprojekten. 2016–2017 Geschäftsführer von Spacespot. Von 2018 bis 2020 Chefredaktor von Modulør.

Born in 1974, he studied education and architecture. He worked for three years as a project architect with Staufer & Hasler in Frauenfeld. Subsequently, he was an assistant director at the Hochbauamt of the City of St.Gallen and 2013–2016, a journalist at TEC21. In addition, since 2013 he has been a freelance publicist with articles in various professional journals and daily papers, as well as diverse book projects. 2016–2017, director of Spacespot. From 2018 to 2020 editor-in-chief of Modulør.

CHRISTOPH WIESER
Geboren 1967, studierte Architektur und war Assistent an der ETH Zürich. 2005 Promotion an der ETH Lausanne. 2003–2009 Redaktor der Zeitschrift werk, bauen + wohnen, 2009–2013 Leiter Zentrum/Institut Konstruktives Entwerfen am Departement Architektur, Gestaltung und Bauingenieurwesen der ZHAW in Winterthur. Architekturtheoretiker, Publizist, Forscher und Dozent an schweizerischen Fachhochschulen.

Born in 1967, he studied architecture and was an assistant at the ETH Zurich. Earned his PhD in 2005 from the ETH Lausanne. 2003–2009 he was editor of the werk, bauen + wohnen journal; 2009–2013, head of the Institute for Constructive Design at the School of Architecture, Design, and Civil Engineering (ZHAW) in Winterthur. Architectural theorist, publicist, researcher, and lecturer at various Swiss universities of applied science.

Haus 10, 5. Obergeschoss, Bürobereich / Building 10, 5th floor, office area
Foto / Photo: Georg Aerni

IMPRESSUM / IMPRINT

Herausgeber / Editors: Marko Sauer, Christoph Wieser
Idee und Konzept / Idea and concept: Fawad Kazi,
   Bruno Margreth, Marko Sauer, Christoph Wieser
Grafische Gestaltung / Graphic design: Bruno Margreth
Administration und Sponsoring / Administration and sponsoring:
   Manuela Kazi
Lektorat deutsch / German copyediting: Sandra Leitte
Korrektorat deutsch / German proofreading: Kirsten Thietz
Übersetzung / Translation: Lisa Rosenblatt
Lektorat englisch / English copyediting: Keonaona Peterson
Korrektorat englisch / English proofreading: Colette Forder
Lithografie, Druck und Bindung / Lithography, print, and
   binding: DZA Druckerei zu Altenburg GmbH, Thüringen

© 2021 Fawad Kazi und / and Park Books AG, Zürich
© für die Texte / for the texts: die Autoren / the authors
© für die Pläne / for the plans: Fawad Kazi Architekt GmbH
© für die Ausführungspläne Passerelle S. 37 / for the Implementation plans of aerial walkway p. 37: Schneider Stahlbau AG
© für die Fotografien und Bilder S. / for the photographs
   and images pp.:
   7, 25–32, 34, 35, 38, 41, 45: Florian Brunner
   8, 10, 13, 16, 21, 33, 43, 47, 48, 50, 55, 63: Georg Aerni
   9, 49, 58: Fawad Kazi Architekt GmbH
   14: Bernd und Hilla Becher
   17: Hertha Hurnaus
   18: 2021, ProLitteris, Zürich; Foto / Photo: Nicolai Schneider
   20: Architekturzentrum Wien, Sammlung,
     Foto / Photo: Margherita Spiluttini, Inv. n 1289–32
   46, 51: Daniel Ammann

Park Books AG
Niederdorfstrasse 54
CH-8001 Zürich
Schweiz / Switzerland
www.park-books.com

Park Books wird vom Bundesamt für Kultur mit einem Strukturbeitrag für die Jahre 2021–2024 unterstützt.
Alle Rechte vorbehalten; kein Teil dieses Werks darf in irgendeiner Form ohne vorherige schriftliche Genehmigung des Verlags reproduziert oder unter Verwendung elektronischer Systeme verarbeitet, vervielfältigt oder verbreitet werden.

Park Books is being supported by the Federal Office of Culture with a general subsidy for the years 2021–2024.
All rights reserved; no part of this publication may be reproduced, stored in a retrieval system or transmitted in any form or by any means, electronic, mechanical, photocopying, recording, or otherwise, without the prior written consent of the publisher.

ISBN 978-3-03860-203-3

DANK / ACKNOWLEDGMENTS

Amstein + Walthert AG, Zürich

BKS stromschienen ag, Balsthal

BlessHess AG, Luzern

E3 HLK AG, St.Gallen

Eduard Truninger AG, Zürich

Enz & Partner GmbH Ingenieurbüro für Verkehrswesen, Zürich

ERR Raumplaner AG, St.Gallen

FSB Franz Schneider Brakel GmbH + Co KG, Brakel DE

Grafitec AG, St.Gallen

Hafida Treuhand AG, Zumikon

Hämmerle + Partner GmbH, Zürich

Huber+Monsch AG, St.Gallen

IBG – Institut für Beratungen im Gesundheitswesen, Aarau

Kantonsspital St.Gallen, St.Gallen

Keller + Steiner AG, Fahrwangen

Lista Office Ostschweiz, St.Gallen

MOOS licht ag, Luzern

Reflexion AG, Zürich

Sauter Building Control Schweiz AG, Gossau

Stiftung Ostschweizer Kinderspital, St.Gallen

vetschpartner Landschaftsarchitekten AG, Zürich

Walter Dietsche Baumanagement AG, Chur

WaltGalmarini AG, Zürich

64